PORTLAND IN THREE CENTURIES

Workers line up in 1917 in front of the Portland Knitting Company factory on Southeast Stark, where the Jantzen brand of sportswear was first produced. Before zoning was adopted in 1924, industrial and commercial buildings sometimes appeared along residential streets. The building later housed Electro Scientific Industries during its start-up years and was then adapted as a Quaker Meetinghouse. (Author's collection)

Portland in Three Centuries

THE PLACE AND THE PEOPLE

Carl Abbott

Oregon State University Press, Corvallis

The paper in this book meets the guidelines for permanence and durability of
the Committee on Production Guidelines for Book Longevity of the Council
on Library Resources and the minimum requirements of the American National
Standard for Permanence of Paper for Printed Library Materials Z39.48-1984.

Library of Congress Cataloging-in-Publication Data

Abbott, Carl.
    Portland in three centuries : the place and the people / Carl Abbott.
        p. cm.
    Includes bibliographical references and index.
    ISBN 978-0-87071-613-3 (alk. paper) — ISBN 978-0-87071-644-7 (ebook)
    1. Portland (Or.)—History. I. Title.
    F884.P857A33 2011
    979.5'49--dc23
                                2011019520

Oregon State University Press
121 The Valley Library
Corvallis OR 97331-4501
541-737-3166 • fax 541-737-3170
http://osupress.oregonstate.edu

Contents

Author's Note

In 1985, I authored *Portland: Gateway to the Northwest*, a brief history of the city with historical photographs and images assembled by Ted Van Arsdol. That book has long been out of print. In the meanwhile, a quarter century of research and writing has greatly expanded and enriched our knowledge of Portland and Portlanders.

The present book builds on my earlier work while incorporating the new generation of scholarship. By rough estimate, the bibliography at the end has doubled in length—even without listing every relevant M.A. thesis by Portland State University history students. The sequence of chapters remains the same, but the text has grown by more than a third and the narrative now carries into the twenty-first century.

I want to thank Tanya March for her indefatigable enthusiasm in helping to identify new images to supplement the text. Thanks as well to Norman Gholston and Thomas Robinson for making many of the images available for my use; to Brian Johnson, Mary Hansen, and the staff of the Portland Archives and Records Center for their great help; to Meg Merrick of the Institute for Portland Metropolitan Studies at Portland State University for help with several maps; to the Oregon Historical Society; and to Robert Johnston and Murase Associates for permission to use individual images.

Readers will also find more and different sorts of people in the story. There are still plenty of politicians and business leaders, for we can't tell the story of Portland without William Ladd and Edgar Kaiser, George Baker and Vera Katz. But there are also more workers and immigrants, more union members and dissenters, more women at work and women in the public realm, more artists and more activists.

Millions of individuals have made the city of Portland and the surrounding region their home for a few years or for decades. By a quick back-of-the-envelope calculation, Portlanders have lived something like 12 billion person-days in the 165 years since the founding of their European American city. When one recalls that it took James Joyce hundreds of pages to cover a single day's worth of Leopold Bloom's activities and thoughts, it is clear that no single book can do justice to such a rich mosaic of experience. I hope, nevertheless, that *Portland in Three Centuries* can help us understand the web of opportunities and problems that have helped to shape those intertwining lives.

Prologue
Gateway to the Northwest

Our great-great-grandparents were quick to credit divine providence for the growth of their cities. The Creator, said one early Chicagoan, had marked the inevitable destiny of that city by rolling back the waves of Lake Michigan. The great bend of the Missouri River seemed a heaven-sent guarantee for the success for Kansas City. Whether Louisville or St. Paul, Toledo or Tacoma, every city seemed to have been foreordained.

In the case of Portland, the general idea was clear enough. There seemed no doubt that a major center of commerce would develop *someplace* along the lower Columbia River between the Cascade Range and the Pacific Ocean. The only problem was exactly *where* that place would be. It was not until 1843 and 1844—after 50 years of Anglo-American exploration and thousands of years of occupancy by American Indian peoples—that a permanent settlement was founded at what would become the middle of downtown Portland, and it would take another decade for the new town to fight off local challengers along the Willamette and Columbia.

More than any of its larger West Coast rivals—Seattle, Tacoma, San Francisco, and Los Angeles—Portland is indeed "the city that gravity built," to repeat the phrase of historian Glenn Quiett. It sits at the crossroads of two lowland corridors that the forces of geological change have stamped onto the landscape of western America. From north to south, more than two-thirds of the population of the Pacific Northwest is found along a 500-mile trough between the volcanic peaks of the Cascades and the string of coastal mountains that extends from the redwood country of northern California to the spine of Vancouver Island. South of the Columbia, the Willamette River flows through the trough. Farther north, the Cowlitz River extends the lowland through Washington State to Puget Sound, which connects in turn to the Strait of Georgia. A string of "Cascadian" cities runs from Eugene, Salem, and Portland in Oregon, through Olympia, Tacoma, Seattle, and Bellingham in Washington, and on to Vancouver and Victoria in British Columbia.

The Columbia River crosses the lowland axis after breaking through the Cascade range 160 miles from the Pacific. The size of its drainage basin and volume of flow are a close match to Europe's greatest river, the Danube. As soon as the Columbia became known to eastern Americans, it entered their dreams as the sure route to the western coast—the "North American road to India" in the words of Missouri Senator Thomas Hart Benton.

Later Portland boosters talked as if the divine hand had not only pointed out the general location for Oregon's metropolis but had actually staked out its exact spot. In sober fact, as we have said, it took explorers and pioneers half a century to hit on the precise spot.

The English-speaking discoverer of the Columbia River was the American trader Robert Gray. His ship, the *Columbia Rediviva*, entered the river's mouth in May 1792, but Gray showed no interest in venturing upstream. Five months later, Lieutenant James Broughton of the British navy, sailing with Captain James Vancouver on the expedition that first mapped Puget Sound, directed the first actual exploration of the lower Columbia. In October 1792, Broughton took the 135-ton *Chatham* across the dangerous Columbia bar and spent three weeks exploring in small boats. He reached the Sandy River and claimed the region for England. Although he noted the confluence of the Willamette, he was more interested in enjoying the scenery and naming Mount Hood for a British admiral.

A dozen years later, Meriwether Lewis, William Clark, and their companions on the transcontinental expedition of 1804–06 missed the mouth of the Willamette not once, but twice. Hurrying downstream in November 1805, they hugged the north bank, so what they called Image Canoe Island (Tomahawk and Hayden islands) blocked their view. On their return after a winter at Fort Clatsop, the expedition reached the Quicksand (Sandy) River before Clark doubled back with an Indian guide to find the Multnomah River, his name for the Willamette. On April 3, 1806, Clark paddled several miles up the Willamette and camped at an unoccupied Indian village somewhere between what is now Terminal 4 and the St. Johns Bridge.

The next day the group proceeded past a point of land on the east bank. Clark's rough estimate of distance supports the idea that he reached the bluff now occupied by the University of Portland, where the river turned sharply around the east side of Swan Island. The mist that morning was too thick to venture farther, but Clark turned around "being perfectly satisfied of the size

Willamette Falls, 15 miles above Portland, was a barrier to transportation on the Willamette River, a valuable fishing site, and a dividing point between the native peoples of the lower Columbia River and those of the Willamette Valley. The Hudson's Bay Company established a trading post in 1829. Oregon City, laid out in 1842, became the primary town for American settlers in the first few years of the Oregon Trail migration. (Photo by Al Monner, courtesy Thomas Robinson)

and magnitude of this great river which must water that vast tract of Country between the western range of mountains and those on the sea coast."

One reason that Clark and other explorers failed to remark on the site that would be the future heart of Portland was because the location was relatively important to the region's Indians. When European and American fur traders began to arrive in the Pacific Northwest at the end of the 1700s, Chinook-speaking people dominated the Columbia from The Dalles to the sea. The Lower Chinooks, among whom Lewis and Clark spent the winter of 1805–06, lived around the wide Columbia estuary. Upstream were the Cathlamets and then the Multnomahs from the Cowlitz River to the Willamette. Their greatest concentration was on and around Sauvie Island. Lewis and Clark counted 2,400 Multnomahs living on the island in several winter villages and an equal number nearby across Multnomah Channel and around Vancouver Lake. Six years later, British fur trader Robert Stuart reported a population of 2,000 on the island—roughly twice the permanent population today.

Twenty-five miles up the Willamette were other Indians who also spoke Chinook dialects. The Clackamas groups were the largest, with perhaps a

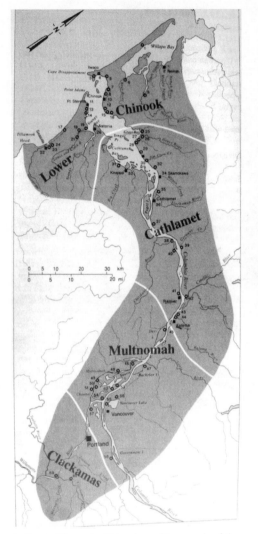

Indian settlements. Chinook-speaking people of the lower Columbia and Willamette rivers lived in a mix of permanent villages and temporary camps clustered in areas where fish, waterfowl, and plants such as wapato were in greatest abundance. This map is from the authoritative *Handbook of North American Indians* published by the Smithsonian Institution.

dozen villages along the river that now bears their name. Smaller bands included the Cushoks and Chahcowahs, who clustered around the falls at the present site of Oregon City. Both the falls and the mouth of the Clackamas were places where it was easy to take salmon, attracting a population of perhaps 2,500.

In the Willamette Valley above the falls were the Kalapuyas, a people distinct from the various branches of Chinooks. They belonged to at least a dozen bands with defined territories. Closest to present-day Portland were the Tualatins, in what is now Washington County. They lived in as many as 15 winter villages, which were self-governing but shared common hunting territories.

Compared to native peoples in many other parts of the continent, the people of the lower Columbia enjoyed a relatively rich and easy life. Lewis and Clark remarked on the special fertility of the Columbia Valley in the vicinity of Portland. The Multnomahs, Clackamas, and other groups in the Portland basin fished for salmon, sturgeon, and smelt; hunted migratory birds and deer that thrived in the riverside woods and clearings; gathered nuts and berries; and dug wapato roots out of muddy marshes to eat raw or roasted. Clark compared the root to the Irish potato and commented that "it has an agreeable taste and answers very well in place of bread." The abundance of wapato gave Sauvie Island its earlier name and supported its especially dense population.

Cedar logs provided the materials for dugout canoes, cooking utensils, and gabled longhouses made of vertical planks lashed to a frame of poles and posts. Usually built over a shallow pit two to six feet deep, the plank lodges might reach a hundred feet in length, with woven mats subdividing the interior space. Households varied in size, but fifty people per house is a very rough approximation. When they traveled to summer hunting and fishing grounds, the Chinooks used temporary shelters made of poles covered with mats and hides.

Their settlements ranged from clusters of a few small houses to substantial villages with hundreds of residents. Each village was an independent entity, bound together by complex kinship ties and represented by one of several headmen. Although the Chinook-speaking villages acknowledged some common connection, each was closer to an independent extended family than part of a larger political unit. They built their villages to last for years, not generations, for the abundance of resources made it easy for bands to move from one spot to another within their general territory. Members of groups along the Columbia visited, intermarried, shared food-gathering sites, and fought for resources and prestige.

In the Chinook economy, the centers of trade were the mouth of the Columbia and the great barrier of Celilo Falls near the present-day city of The Dalles. Where the Columbia met the sea, the Chinook traded with other coastal peoples and, after Robert Gray and James Broughton visited, with European and American sailing ships. Celilo Falls was the dividing point between the lush coastal lands and the dry ranges and plateaus of the interior. It was also the boundary between the lifestyle of the Northwest coast and that of inland tribes such as the Shoshonis, Paiutes, and Nez Perce. Both before and after the arrival of British fur traders, the break in navigation on the Columbia made The Dalles a natural market and a "general theater of gambling and roguery" in the critical view of one trader. The Multnomahs and other tribes near the lower Willamette lived along the artery of trade but controlled neither of the key points of exchange.

The Chinooks were eager and natural trading partners for British and American fur companies. Both "King George's men" and "Boston men" took two years to make a round-the-world circuit with stops at the Northwest coast, the Hawaiian Islands, and China. The heyday of maritime commerce to the Columbia lasted from 1792 until the War of 1812. Thereafter, attention focused on transcontinental trade. New Yorker John Jacob Astor organized the Pacific Fur Company in 1810 and planted the trading post that evolved into the city of Astoria. Three years later he sold out to the North West Company, a Montreal-based firm that renamed the post Fort George and dominated regional fur trade until 1821.

In turn, the powerful British Hudson's Bay Company swallowed up the North West Company. Fort George soon dwindled to a lookout post to

report on possible competition and the Hudson's Bay operations moved to
Fort Vancouver, built in 1825 on the north shore of the Columbia, seven miles
upstream from the Willamette. Under the leadership of John McLoughlin,
the new settlement was the focal point of a Columbia Basin trading network
extending hundreds of miles into the interior.

Fewer than thirty years after Lewis and Clark brought back reports
of the Chinooks and Kalapuyas, and less than a decade after the building of
Fort Vancouver, disease had virtually exterminated the native population of
northwestern Oregon. The spread of the Anglo-American trading system
opened the possibility of both immediate economic gains and ultimate ca-
tastrophe for Indians. Among the world's most isolated peoples, the Indians
of the Northwest Coast were easily susceptible to new diseases that arrived
with Europeans. Smallpox had come upriver in 1780, 1801–02, and 1824–25,
and had already reduced the Indian population. Now the "Cold Sick" or "In-
termitting Fever" appeared in Chinook and Kalapuya villages in 1829–30 and
raged for the next three years. Circumstantial evidence suggests that the disease was malaria, brought from the tropics by traders. The Cold Sick spread
outward from an infection epicenter at Sauvie Island and Fort Vancouver. It
killed half the inhabitants in some villages and 90 percent in others, leaving
only a few hundred Native Americans and a virtually unoccupied Lower
Columbia and Willamette Valley landscape. Observed from the outside and
in retrospect, the Cold Sick was a tragedy whose human cost we can scarcely
calculate.

The first European and American settlers who filled the void also ignored the site of Portland. Fort Vancouver continued to be the major British
settlement, humming with activity that impressed occasional visitors. It was
a cosmopolitan settlement—officials in 1827 counted 157 "whites and half
breeds," 20 "owyhees" from the Hawaiian Islands, 13 "natives," and 4 Iro-
quois from eastern Canada. Fort William, a rival trading post built on Sauvie
Island by the independent American fur trader Nathaniel Wyeth, lasted only
two years, from 1835 to 1837, before the Hudson's Bay Company turned the
abandoned site into a dairy farm. Hall J. Kelley, an eccentric New Englander
who dedicated his life to fervently boosting Oregon, proposed to establish
a "commercial town . . . about two miles square" at the juncture of the Willamette and Columbia. According to his crudely sketched map, the city was to
run across the North Portland peninsula from Smith Lake and the Columbia
Slough to the St. Johns neighborhood. We are scarcely surprised that the proposal sank without a trace, since Kelley had picked the site years before his
brief and highly unsuccessful visit to Oregon in 1834 and 1835.

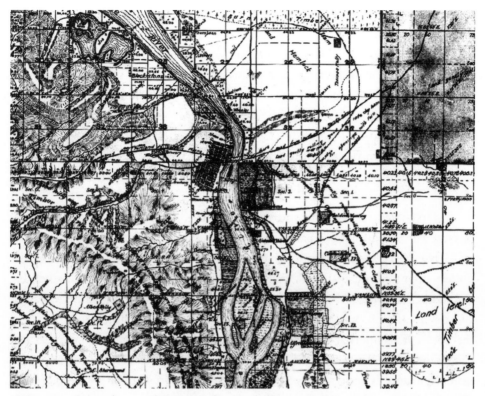

1852 survey map. Key features of the early Portland landscape are still obvious today, such as the West Hills, the volcanic cones of the east side, and the line of the Alameda ridge. Many of the smaller details of older wetlands and smaller streams, however, have been obscured by landfill and other efforts to smooth the original topography. (Portland State University, Institute for Portland Metropolitan Studies)

Early traders and settlers who followed the Willamette upstream from Fort Vancouver in the 1830s or early 1840s had their eyes on the falls or the interior valley beyond. Their diaries and reports usually ignored or dismissed the first few miles of the river, where Portland was eventually to be built. The banks were either high bluffs or low and swampy ground, and the land behind was too thickly wooded for quick and easy cultivation. Philadelphia physician and naturalist John Townsend summed up the common reaction when he wrote that "there is not a sufficient extent unencumbered, or which could be fitted for the purposes of tillage in a space of time short enough to be serviceable; others are at some seasons inundated, which is an insurmountable objection."

As a result, the first large European settlements along the Willamette itself were upstream from the site of Portland. Retired employees of the Hudson's Bay Company, mostly French Canadians, began to settle and cultivate the "French Prairie" in 1829. By 1840–41, the community had grown to more than sixty families, who worshipped in a new Roman Catholic church and sold their surplus wheat to Fort Vancouver through a small warehouse and landing at Champoeg, 25 miles above Willamette Falls. A second settlement formed at the base of the falls, where John McLoughlin and Methodist missionaries contended for control of what seemed to be a natural location for a major town. Rival development efforts started in 1840 and 1841. By the winter of 1842–43, the new community of Oregon City had made a significant impression on the wilderness, with more than thirty buildings, a gristmill, and growing competition for building lots. It was the first destination for most of the participants in the swelling American migrations that had brought more than eight hundred settlers to Oregon in 1843 and about twelve hundred more in 1844.

Into the early 1840s, in short, the history of Portland is a story of near misses. The Chinooks preferred to live at Sauvie Island or along the Clackamas River and traded at the mouth of the Columbia and at Celilo Falls. British traders operated out of Fort Vancouver with satellite operations at Sauvie Island and Champoeg. Missionaries followed Indians into the Willamette Valley and up the Columbia, while American settlers made Oregon City their first real town. The site that would become Portland, meanwhile, remained at the beginning of 1843 what it had been before—a small clearing of an acre of so made by trappers and Indians traveling between Fort Vancouver and Oregon City. It served as a sort of early highway rest area where travelers could rest or cook a midday meal during the 30-mile trip. Jesse A. Applegate later described the site he had visited as a boy in 1843:

> We landed on the west shore and went into camp on the high bank where there was little underbrush . . . No one lived there and the place had no name; there was nothing to show that the place had ever been visited except a small log hut near the river, and a broken mast of a ship leaning against the high bank. There were chips hewn from timber, showing that probably a new mast had been made there. . . . We were then actually encamped on the site of the city of Portland, but there was no prophet with us to tell of the beautiful city that was to take the place of the gloomy forest.

Chapter 1
Stumptown

The Pacific Northwest was an international trouble spot in 1845. Political control of the Oregon Country—what is now Idaho, Oregon, Washington, and British Columbia—had been in dispute since the eighteenth century. England and the United States had pushed Russian claims north to Alaska and Spanish claims south to California in the first quarter of the nineteenth century and had then settled down to a diplomatic marathon that lasted from president to president and prime minister to prime minister. Along the lower Columbia, the two sides traced their land claims to the 1792 voyages of Gray and Broughton.

Tension had mounted rapidly during the presidential campaign of 1844, when the issue of American control of Oregon helped to put Democrat James K. Polk in the White House. The growing American settlements along the Willamette and Columbia rivers were upsetting the delicate balance of commercial interests worked out by the men of the Hudson's Bay Company, and the British government correctly feared that Polk would cancel the joint occupancy agreement that had given citizens of both nations free access to Oregon since 1818.

In 1845, the British military command in Canada dispatched Lieutenants Henry Warre and M. Vavasour from Montreal for a military reconnaissance of this hot spot. They traveled openly under the joint occupancy agreement in the guise of "private individuals, seeking amusement." Their real job was to scout out possible locations for coastal defenses, sea batteries, and river fortifications in case Britain decided to hold the territory against the Americans. Their report from Fort Vancouver in October 1845 counted the surviving Chinooks, Kalapuyas, and Klickitats; described the American settlements; and suggested that a small British force stationed at Oregon City "would overawe the present American population" of three hundred. The only other settlement they noted on the lower Willamette was one family at Linnton.

Oregon City. Lieutenant Henry J, Warre of the Royal Engineers, on a reconnaissance of Oregon for the British, sketched the new American settlement at Oregon City as of 1845-46. As the first large English-speaking town and initial territorial capital, Oregon City was Portland's first rival as the new metropolis of the West. (Gholston collection)

Warre and Vavasour's second report on June 16, 1846, mentioned a new town. "Since the summer," they wrote their superiors, "a village called Portland has been commenced between the falls and Linnton, to which an American merchant ship ascended and discharged her cargo, in September." After struggling with their canoes through high water and willow swamps and camping on muddy beaches for more than a year, the two British officers were impressed by dry land. "The situation of Portland is superior to that of Linnton, and the back country of easier access. There are several settlements on the banks of the river, below the falls, but the water, covering the low lands during the freshets, renders them valueless for cultivation, and but few situations can be found adapted for building on."

Neither the British travelers nor the handful of Portlanders knew that exactly three days after Warre and Vavasour sealed their second dispatch, the United States Senate was making their mission irrelevant by ratifying the Anglo-American Oregon Treaty. The compromise boundary was the 49th parallel from the Rocky Mountains to Puget Sound, and from there around the south end of Vancouver Island and through the Strait of Juan de Fuca to the open Pacific. The future states of Idaho, Washington, and Oregon became the undisputed territory of the United States.

Portland was two and a half years old when the new treaty officially made it an "all American" town. The burgeoning settlement was the result of a bright idea by a drifter named William Overton. Overton spent two years off and on in Oregon before he spotted the clearing along the west bank of the Willamette. In November 1843, he showed the site to Asa Lovejoy, an Oregon City lawyer, and the two became co-owners of the 640 acres that would become downtown Portland when they filed a claim with the settlers' provisional government at Oregon City early in 1844. Lovejoy took a half-interest in the property when he agreed to pay the 25-cent filing fee. The men were claiming presumptive title, awaiting official acquisition of the territory by the United States and a procedure for distributing land to Oregon pioneers.

Portland's founding father quickly lost interest in his land speculation. Overton left Oregon to try his fortunes in California and, in the spring of 1844, sold out to Francis Pettygrove, a leading Oregon City merchant, for a $50 grubstake. Later that year, Pettygrove and Lovejoy hired a man to enlarge the clearing at the Willamette and build a cabin; he soon complained that the mosquitoes were so thick he couldn't work outside and that fleas made the inside of the cabin just as intolerable.

The next year brought the property both a name and a survey. But for the toss of a coin, the town would have been called Boston, not Portland. Co-owner Asa Lovejoy was from Massachusetts and held a degree from Amherst College; he liked the idea of owning half of "Boston." Pettygrove hailed from the state of Maine and wanted to name the town "Portland." They "snapped up a copper," to use Lovejoy's words, and Pettygrove won the toss. That same year the speculators hired surveyor Thomas Brown to stake out blocks and lots so they could sell their property to new settlers. The original plat was two blocks deep and eight wide, bounded by Front, Second, Washington, and Jefferson. There were eight 50-by-100-foot lots on each small block.

Though Portland seemed well on its way to becoming a real community, Lovejoy, like his former partner Overton, lost interest in the townsite. Beckoned by politics, Lovejoy decided in November 1845 that his future lay in Oregon City, the territorial capital, and sold his half interest in Portland to Benjamin Stark, cargo-master on the bark *Toulon*. Stark had dealt with Pettygrove in the trade between New York and Portland. Since Stark spent much of his time sailing back and forth to Oahu, finally settling down to a prosperous life in San Francisco, Pettygrove found himself responsible not only for the name but also for the future of Portland.

What historian Eugene Snyder has called "Portland's Pettygrove period" lasted for two years, during which the settlement underwent steady but unremarkable growth. Before the summer of 1846 was over, about sixty residents occupied Portland's first 12 to 15 houses. James Terwilliger shoed horses at First and Morrison. Daniel Lownsdale's tannery was out of town to the west, where a creek flowed from the hills past the present site of Jeld-Wen Field. The center of town was Francis Pettygrove's store and wharf at the foot of Washington Street. A rough and rutted wagon track ran from the wharf past Lownsdale's tannery to the "Twality Plains."

By the summer of 1847, the town had grown to about a hundred people. J. Q. Thornton, an early Oregon judge, described the place as having "an air of neatness, thrift, and industry." Sophisticates from larger towns like Oregon City were not always so kind. Although the trees had been cleared from rights-of-way to show where the streets had been surveyed, many of the stumps remained. Some were whitewashed to prevent nighttime wanderers from tripping. It was hard for outsiders to resist giving the place the nickname "Stumptown."

California's Gold Rush brought both crisis and opportunity for Stumptown. The news of James Marshall's discovery of gold at Sutter's Mill near Sacramento arrived in August. Thousands of Oregonians caught gold fever. They hurried south to reach the Sierras before the snows and to get a jump on the expected hordes of prospectors from the East. Among the gold-seekers were dozens of families from Portland. According to popular lore, the town's population was reduced to a grand total of three people. Francis Pettygrove bartered his half ownership of Portland to Daniel Lownsdale for $5,000 worth of leather, and liquidated his other assets in Oregon before sailing to San Francisco early in 1849. There he sold Lownsdale's leather to '49ers at a healthy profit. People who stayed in Portland also made good money by supplying lumber and food, primarily wheat, for the California market. The supplies were sent by ship down the Willamette and Columbia rivers, then down the coast to San Francisco. On one day in midsummer 1849, twenty ships were loading in the lower Willamette at the same time. The volume of Oregon exports increased by fivefold in that year.

However, one summer of trade does not make a city. "Why Portland?" was the question that every smart investor and newly arrived merchant should have asked at the beginning of 1850. Stumptown would grow only if its economy was based on a solid foundation. Two "generations" of Portland promoters—Overton and Lovejoy, Pettygrove and Stark—had already given up on Portland to seek greener pastures. Half a dozen rival settlements along a 50-mile stretch of the lower Willamette and Columbia offered serious

Front Street. Portland in its earliest years looked like a Western movie set, with false-front buildings, muddy streets, and merchants searching the town for business. (Portland City Archives)

competition, and fortunes changed fast on the frontier. Would Portland or Milwaukie be the metropolis of Oregon? Milton City or Oregon City? St. Johns or St. Helens, or some site still unnamed?

The competition between Portland and its rival settlements in the early 1850s is a fairly typical chapter in the familiar story of American townsite promotion. As settlement moved west in the nineteenth century, speculators rushed to claim every promising harbor, ford, or dry stretch of riverfront. A cynical British observer had previously described the process in the Mississippi Valley:

> A speculator makes out a plan of a city with its streets, squares, and avenues, quays and wharves, public buildings and monuments. The streets are lotted, the houses numbered, and the squares called after Franklin or Washington. The city itself has some fine name, perhaps Troy or Antioch . . . All this time the city is a mere vision . . .500 miles beyond civilization, probably under water or surrounded by dense forests and impassable swamps.

This ambitious platting of towns occurred across the young United States. The towns that managed to attract more than a handful of settlers plunged into a struggle for reputation and trade. There were half a dozen aspiring Toledos in northwestern Ohio in the 1830s. Chicago had to contend with the ambitions of Waukegan. At the same time that Portland was scrambling for its future, Kansas City was fighting Atchison and Leavenworth to be the metropolis of the Missouri. Closer to home, Portlanders would soon be able to watch Tacoma, Seattle, and Everett compete to be the major city and chief port on Puget Sound.

In Oregon, the ostensible issue in 1850 was the location of the "head of navigation," the point of closest access by ocean shipping to the agricultural riches of the Willamette Valley. As every sailor knew, there was actually no such definitive point. The head of navigation varied with the season, the length of the wharf, the type of ship, and the courage or foolishness of its captain. Every town could legitimately advance some claim to the title. The real question was which town had the most *push*—a wonderful word that meant ambition, boosterism, and canny entrepreneurship to our great-great-grandparents.

Portland eventually took the prize because it had the most skilled and persistent promoters. Daniel Lownsdale had divided his share of Portland with two new partners during the course of 1849. Stephen Coffin of Maine, an energetic building contractor who had come to Oregon City in 1847, and William Chapman of Virginia, a lawyer who had made money in the California Gold Rush, provided ideas, energy, and capital. During two momentous years in 1850 and 1851, Portland's triumvirate provided three essentials that assured their town's permanent growth—dependable steamship service to California, the Great Plank Road across the West Hills, and promotion of the town in the form of the purple prose of the *Oregonian* newspaper.

A newspaper on the nineteenth-century frontier was vitally important, serving as a sort of urban identification card. Like a post office or a county courthouse, even a four-page weekly was accepted proof that a townsite was a going concern. It rankled and grated the city's leadership in the early months of 1850 that Portland merchants had to advertise their wares in Oregon City's *Spectator.* Chapman and Coffin remedied the situation by recruiting an unemployed editor with a battered hand-printing press from San Francisco. Thomas Jefferson Dryer arrived in November, his equipment a month later. The first issue of the *Oregonian* appeared on December 4, 1850.

Dryer ran the paper for ten years. He advocated the Whig and then the Republican party, boosted the city of Portland, and used every printable insult in the language in feuds with Salem's *Oregon Statesman* and Portland's second newspaper, the *Democratic Standard*, which was published from 1854 to 1859. The typical weekly issue of the *Oregonian* in the 1850s was a combination of newspaper, *Reader's Digest*, and telephone yellow pages. The first page carried short fiction, jokes, articles copied from Eastern papers, and the equivalent of today's wire service filler. The back page and one of the interior pages carried business cards and advertisements from firms in Portland, Oregon City, and more distant towns like Albany and Olympia. The listings, which scarcely varied from month to month, functioned as a business directory. The other inside page contained editorials and "Latest News by the Mail" from San Francisco.

If the *Oregonian* gave Portland equal standing with Oregon City as an information center for the territory, then a few miles of unfinished plank road were enough for Portland to gain victory over the town's nearest rivals. At the start of the 1850s, Americans throughout the Midwest and South were seized by a mania for plank roads—highways with a surface of sawed planks spiked to wooden stringers. They were touted as "the farmers' railroad," easy for amateurs to build and almost as cheap as dirt in the states around the Great Lakes and in the Northwest, where lumber was virtually free for the cutting.

The territorial legislature chartered the Portland and Valley Plank Road Company in January 1851. The organizational meeting was held in Lafayette, but Portland's "Big Three" of Lownsdale, Coffin, and Chapman signed up to buy a third of the stock, and the construction started southwestward from Portland. The route led up the ravine of Tanner Creek, over the Sylvan hill, and on to its final destination of Hillsborough. Work on the roadbed started in late summer. The first planks, from Portland's own steam sawmill, went down with great fanfare and suitable oratory on September 27, 1851. The company ran out of money after planking only a few miles of this first version of Canyon Road, but even the rutted track that continued into the rich agricultural lands of the Tualatin Valley made Portland the most accessible port for Washington County farmers, who shipped their abundant wheat to San Francisco.

Portland's plank road doomed the already fading hopes of Linnton. Linnton's founders were Morton McCarver, a "compulsive town promoter" in the words of historian Malcolm Clark, Jr., and Peter Burnett, a frontier lawyer who had come to Oregon ahead of his creditors and who eventually became the first governor of the State of California. They had staked out the town in 1844 at the end of an old cattle trail that the Hudson's Bay men at Vancouver had used to move their cattle to summer pastures in the Tualatin country. The developers planned to turn the cattle trail into a real road, but never did, and few farmers bothered to ship their wheat through the Linnton warehouse. The California Gold Rush took Linnton's last residents as they headed south to seek their fortunes, and the Portland plank road killed any hopes of the town's revival.

Cazeno or Baker's Landing or Springville—it took a while to settle on a name—was a slightly more successful town located a mile upstream at what is now the west end of the St. Johns Bridge. Washington County cut a road through the hills in 1852 to give wheat farmers and stockmen on its northern edge an alternative route to the Willamette. One result was a new community that grew up around the warehouse at the Willamette terminus of the road. This small settlement of Springville helped to fill ships that sometimes left Portland half empty. We have no population count, but the site was important enough to be designated as a post office around 1860. By the early 1870s, however, the warehouse had burned and the town and its road had fallen out of use.

Milwaukie and St. Johns, located on the Willamette's east side, were on the wrong side of the river to profit from the development of Washington County agriculture. James Johns had claimed a square mile of land and laid out a town at the end of the 1840s. By 1851 St. Johns had a dozen families, but it was too isolated to prosper. There was more uncleared forest than farmland on the east side of the river and therefore little business for the town. The "ferry" to Linnton was a rowboat. The settlement would have a renaissance as an independent port and city around 1900, but it was not a serious contender in the competition among the region's towns in the early 1850s.

Milwaukie had been founded by Lot Whitcomb in 1848. Whitcomb built sailing ships to carry lumber to the California market at great profit and published the *Western Star*, whose first issue went to press two weeks ahead of the *Oregonian*. He also built a side-wheeled steamboat named for himself. The *Lot Whitcomb of Oregon* went into service in February 1851 on a regular run to Portland, St. Helens, the mouth of the Cowlitz River, Cathlamet, Astoria, and back. The steamer had a 140-horsepower engine and clocked an impressive 14 miles per hour. It was also painfully expensive to operate. By June, Whitcomb was forced to sell his namesake to a syndicate of Oregon City investors.

Milwaukie was a good place to load lumber but, like St. Johns, was isolated and inconvenient for Washington County wheat growers. Ships reached Milwaukie without trouble during the spring floods. During the winter of 1850–51, however, one after another scraped bottom on the Ross Island sandbar that lay between Portland and Milwaukie. Indeed, Captain John H. Couch, the New England seaman and merchant who had made Portland his base of operations in 1849, announced to the public that the river at Ross

Island ordinarily had "only about four feet of water." He had himself ridden across on horseback at Ross Island and did not think that Milwaukie would ever overcome the handicap created by the shallows. Most embarrassing of all for Milwaukie, the editor of the *Western Star* (who had gained ownership when Whitcomb ran out of cash) moved his business to Portland, where he printed the first copies of the *Oregon Weekly Times* on June 5. "In removing from Milwaukie to Portland," he announced, "we have been guided by those considerations which govern all business men."

Portland's promoters matched their rivals sawmill for sawmill, editor for editor, and boat for boat. In San Francisco, Coffin and Chapman had found more than editor T. J. Dryer—they had also found the steamer *Gold Hunter*, which arrived on the first day of December 1850 after they convinced the captain to sail to Portland with the idea of selling an interest in the ship. The San Francisco owners wanted $60,000 in order to transfer control. Steamboats were important because they could navigate the turns of the Willamette more easily than sailing ships, which preferred to stay in the Columbia. Several citizens of Portland decided to invest in the steamer, with Coffin taking the largest share. The *Gold Hunter* was a side-wheeler like the *Lot Whitcomb*. It was only 12 feet longer but much broader, displacing 510 tons to the 300 displaced by the pride of Milwaukie. Most important, the *Gold Hunter* ran not just to Astoria but to San Francisco, giving Portland a sort of presumptive equality with the metropolis of the West. But the *Gold Hunter* made only four round trips before past debts and old creditors surfaced in California and squeezed out the Portland owners.

Though the *Gold Hunter* was a financial failure, it was a speculative success because its service from San Francisco prompted California merchants to say "Portland" when they meant "Oregon." This helped fend off Portland's last and potentially most serious rival, St. Helens. Eugene Snyder has summarized the situation by stating that Portland fought two battles with St. Helens and its satellite of Milton City: "one battle was fought over the wagons; the other battle was for the ships." St. Helenites built a road over the Cornelius Pass in 1850, but Portland countered successfully with the Great Plank Road. In February 1852, the Pacific Mail Steamship Company announced that its California–Oregon service would terminate at St. Helens. Portland had not been chosen as terminus since the company was concerned about the sandbar at Swan Island, which threatened to hamper navigation at Portland just as the Ross Island bar had done at Milwaukie. Two years later, however, Portland's population of a thousand, and its plank road, proved too much for tiny St. Helens. And, with Portland still served by sailing ships and occasional steamers, the Pacific Mail found it hard to make full cargoes at St. Helens. At the start of 1854, Pacific Mail advertised to San Franciscans that its Oregon service would terminate at Portland.

The maps and notes from federal land surveyors in 1852 offer a fascinating snapshot of the countryside that would turn into Portland's neighborhoods. The early version of Sandy Boulevard was already on the map, as was a meandering version of Powell-Foster. North-south trails bent to the east around the barrier of Sullivan's Gulch. The surveyors noted where the soil was good, described the tree cover (mostly fir, hemlock, and maple), and mapped two stretches of "burnt timber" above the Alameda Ridge and in outer Southeast.

Emigrants to Oregon Territory took up land under the Donation Land Claim Act, which was in effect from 1850 to 1855. The law allowed single men to claim 320 acres at no charge and each member of a married couple to claim 320 acres in his and her own names. Nearly 7,500 grants were recorded for the entire territory (including the future Washington and Idaho as well as Oregon). Settlers who picked farm sites under the act had particular criteria. They liked land that had access to water that could be navigated by small boats, but that was not too swampy and waterlogged to cultivate. In the larger area around Portland, that meant the French Prairie near Champoeg and land in the Yamhill, Tualatin, and Clackamas river valleys. Closer to the new city, Johnson Creek, Fanno Creek, and the Columbia Slough all attracted clusters of claims, while higher tracts were less popular. On the east side in particular, trees were coming down, stumps were under attack, fields were being plowed, and fruit tree seedlings were being turned into orchards.

The banks of the major rivers themselves were less attractive than the smaller streams. There were a few spots where dry land sloped directly to the river, such as Fort Vancouver, Linnton, St. Johns, Sellwood, and Milwaukie, but large stretches of riverfront consisted of low sandy islands, separated by shallow channels from tangled bottomlands and backed by rising hills or bluffs, such as Ross Island–Oaks Bottom and Swan Island–Mock's Bottom. Marshes fronted the banks where streams reached the Willamette through Sullivan's Gulch, Marquam Gulch, and the creeks that flowed through what are now the Brooklyn and Hawthorne/Buckman neighborhoods. Two large sets of seasonally flooded lakes covered long shelves of low-lying riverfront land. One stretched six miles along the west shore of the Willamette starting with Couch's Lake and continuing northwestward through Guild's Lake, Kittredge Lake, and Doane's Lake. The second was along the south shore of the Columbia between the river and the slough, where during seasonal flooding Smith and Bybee lakes covered an area six or eight times as large as they do today.

With transportation by land and water and a newspaper editor to tell the world about its increasing success as a trade center, it was time to turn the settlement of Portland into a city. The territorial legislature issued Portland's municipal charter early in 1851, incorporating 2.1 square miles of Douglas fir forest, stumps, and houses as the city of Portland. In the city's first election, held the same year, Portland's male citizens chose Hugh O'Bryant as mayor and five other residents as city councilmen to serve the fledgling metropolis. Their main function seems to have been to keep the city in business. During their first months in office they established systems for assessing property, collecting taxes, recording city finances, selling business licenses, recording their own deliberations, and conducting elections. The first bill paid from the city treasury came to $29.65 (three brass candlesticks at one dollar each and a box of whale oil candles). In 1854, the territorial legislature created a separate Multnomah County with Portland as county seat.

By the time such recognizable names as Josiah Failing and William S. Ladd begin to appear on the list of mayors (elected in 1853 and 1854, respectively), the city had started to keep the peace and to lift its residents out of the mud. There were ordinances for abating nuisances, licenses for vehicles, and a town jail. Ordinance No. 20 required that "all male persons over the age of 21 years" devote two days a year to working on street improvements, or else pay an equivalent tax. A start was made at planking the most heavily used streets, which one visitor had described as mud and water mixed to "a very good batter." Wooden sidewalks prevented pedestrians from miring down alongside horses and wagons and let the ladies keep their skirts out of the deepest mud.

The town that Mayor O'Bryant and his successors tried to govern was more like a giant fraternity house than a real community. Three-quarters of the 805 residents recorded in the 1850 census were male. Nine-tenths of all Portlanders in their twenties were men, attracted by jobs in road and building construction. When young Elizabeth Miller and four other schoolteachers from New England passed through town in 1851 on the way to new posts in Oregon City, Miller reported that "the one-sided community was exceedingly interested." She speculated that the entire population must have crowded the wharf for a look. Another woman commented tersely that Portland was "rather gamey."

Single women who were not teachers could earn money as seamstresses, making and repairing clothing. They could also keep boardinghouses, putting domestic skills such as cooking and cleaning to work to meet the practical needs of a bachelor society. Such was the case of the fictional Mrs. Greyfield depicted by Francis Fuller Victor in *The New Penelope, and Other Stories*

Dog license receipt. One of the early problems faced by Portland City Council was stray dogs. As one constituent complained, "mongrels and valueless dogs" made it so that "a lady cannot walk the streets without coming in contact with scenes and sights that are revolting and disgusting." The council responded in 1859 with an ordinance charging owners who let their dogs run free a punitive license fee of $2 per quarter-year. (Portland City Archives, Photo A 2001-049)

and Poems. Speaking to an unnamed narrator, Mrs. Greyfield describes her widowhood and the pressures to marry in the Portland of the 1850s. She began her life in Portland sewing in a single rented room and graduated to running a boardinghouse, feeding regular meals to men who "were bachelors, who quartered themselves where they could." The dramatic needs of the story require that she eventually marries a seemingly charming man who turns out to have left a family back in Ohio, but Victor's observations of the realities of early Portland match the experience of settlers in other frontier cities as well.

Over the next decade, Portland's population nearly quadrupled, increasing from 805 to 2,874. Oregon grew even faster as immigrants filled the Willamette Valley and explored the mountains with an eye toward a mineral bonanza like that of California. The city's mix of population set it apart from the rest of the territory. The typical Oregonian in the early 1850s had come from states like Missouri, Illinois, Kentucky, and Indiana in the heart of the Mississippi Valley. In Portland, a much larger proportion hailed from New England and from New York, the number one state of origin. Together, Yankees and New Yorkers constituted more than a quarter of Portland's total population in its early decades. The northeastern states also supplied a disproportionate share of the city's business leaders, many of whom began their careers in the early 1850s as agents or correspondents for New York– and Boston-based mercantile companies.

Portland served as the depot and general store for the growing Oregon population. Visitors usually began their descriptions of the city by tallying the number of businesses—18 "stores" in November 1850, 35 "wholesale and retail stores" in 1852, and a hundred shops by 1858. The census of 1860 counted 146 merchants, ranging from local retailers to prosperous agents for large Eastern wholesalers such as Henry W. Corbett or the Failing family.

Portlanders strung their town along the river. In the first few years of development, any building more than 200 yards inland was likely to be hidden in the trees. John Couch laid out streets on his property parallel and perpendicular to the river, despite the bend that caused them to intersect the original plat at the odd angles that are still present along Burnside and Ankeny streets. Daniel Lownsdale expanded the original survey in 1848 with more than a hundred additional blocks. In 1852 he set aside a narrow strip of 11 park blocks along the western edge of the city, perhaps as a firebreak, and reserved two blocks as public squares between Third and Fourth streets (although the city had to pay for Chapman and Lownsdale squares in 1870 because title had never actually transferred).

In the long term, citizens have been grateful for Lownsdale's foresight, but the earliest Portlanders continued to build on Front, First, and Second. If we can trust a view of the city drawn in 1858, woodcutters and sawmill owners had cleared the forest about half a mile back from the waterfront, leaving the straggling town exposed on bare ground between the river and the hills.

Business centered on the docks, warehouses, and waterfront stores. Commercial buildings were normally two stories tall; four stories was the maximum. The most common materials were locally sawed wood and white paint. But successful merchants followed the lead of Vermonter William S. Ladd, who had arrived in Portland in 1851 and who put up the city's first brick building to house his mercantile business in 1853. Residents lived in old log cabins or new frame houses. Surviving in 2011 were the Hallock and McMillan Building, erected in 1857 at the corner of Front and Oak, the Northrup and Blossom Building of 1858 on Yamhill, and the 1859 Delschneider Building on Oak.

The 1850s saw the emergence of Portland's first business elite. The townsite proprietors, with the exception of John Couch, overextended themselves, took on too much debt, and found it difficult to turn their lots and landholdings into ready cash. At the same time, as historians E. K. MacColl and Harry Stein have analyzed, a handful of Front Street merchants slowly gained dominant positions over competitors. A shrewd business mind and the willingness to keep one's store open from dawn to midnight helped, but so did partners and sources of credit in Boston or San Francisco. Josiah Failing and his son Henry expected to stay only a few years before cashing out and returning east, but they found Portland too full of opportunities to leave. William S. Ladd enjoyed backing from Californian Charles Tilton. George Flanders was John Couch's brother-in-law, and Cicero Lewis married one of the captain's daughters. Other names that topped the list of Portland wealth-holders by 1860 included Philip Wasserman, Henry W. Corbett, and Simeon Reed.

In a city with few families, tax-supported schools were a hard sell to unmarried male voters. Transplanted New Englanders succeeded in organizing a public school district in 1851 and offered classes for two years, although *Oregonian* editor Dryer fulminated against spending a thousand dollars "for pedagogueing some dozen or two of children." The first schoolmaster not only taught school, but also unloaded ships, worked on the streets, and fought the shaking ague between terms. In 1854, the major educational institution in the city was the Methodist-run Portland Academy and Female Seminary, but a reorganized district opened again in 1855 in rented space. Future mayor and Oregon governor Sylvester Pennoyer taught in the new public school for six months until he established a law practice in Portland. There was another gap in public education in 1856 and 1857, but the first public school building, Central School, opened in 1858 at Sixth and Morrison, the present site of Pioneer Courthouse Square. By 1860, 272 students crowded into the three rooms of Central School, while an equal number attended several private schools.

Like every ambitious town on the Western frontier, Portland looked on every new building as a step away from the log cabin and toward to the metropolis. Portlanders were proud of public structures like the Central School and the city jail. Culture came to Portland in 1858 when the Willamette Theater opened on Stark Street. Traveling troupes of second-rate actors from San Francisco could now play to audiences of up to six hundred rather than making do with second-story lecture halls or the Multnomah County Courthouse. Drinking, fighting, and horse racing were also high on the list of amusements.

More proper citizens in the 1850s could join the Sons of Temperance and pledge total abstinence from alcohol. They could attend Sunday services in a new Taylor Street Methodist Church after 1850, a new Congregational church in 1851, and a Roman Catholic church in 1852. Presbyterians and Episcopalians built their churches in mid-decade and Baptists at the beginning of the 1860s. The city's hundred or so Jews organized Congregation Beth Israel in 1858 and finished a synagogue in 1861 at Fifth and Oak, considered at the time to be a remote location.

Clinton Kelly Homestead. Clinton Kelly's extensive land claim along Southeast Powell included the future site of Cleveland High School (it was the Clinton Kelly High School of Commerce until 1948). In 1860 the homestead supported Kentuckian Kelly, his third wife Moriah, six children aged four to seventeen, and six hired hands from Ireland, New York, Connecticut, Michigan, and Illinois—a good indication of the varied sources of Portland early English-speaking residents. This early photograph shows a farm on the Kelly property, with a prize horse posed as proudly as the children.

By the end of the 1850s, something about Portland set it apart from the rowdiest of the West's instant cities. There was money to be made here, but with none of the bonanzas of Nevada's Virginia City or Colorado's Leadville or the overnight fortunes of San Francisco. The New Englanders and New Yorkers who dominated the city's economy cannot be called complacent or sober, but they did treat their business lives as serious business. They also propped open the door of opportunity for anyone who could help the city grow, whether U.S. born or immigrant from Europe. For example, Jewish immigrants like Bernard Goldsmith and Philip Wasserman started prosperous businesses in the 1850s, and each later served two terms as mayor.

Few of Portland's city-builders wanted the life of Daniel Boone or Jim Bridger. They were true conservatives who wanted to reconstruct the society they had left behind while reserving a place for themselves at the head table. By the end of the 1850s, when the town was poised for a new surge of growth, Portlanders had organized a typically American community of churches and schools, government, politics, and fraternal organizations. To most visitors, Portland was a little island of New England on the western margin of the continent—handsome, energetic, steady.

Claimants

When in doubt, you farmed.

That was the United States in 1860, when agricultural employment was the default option. As the storm of civil war gathered, 60 percent of all American workers counted by the national census were farmers and farmhands, not to mention the family members who pitched in to tend livestock, chase chickens out of the garden, churn butter, and mend fences.

It was the same in the wide, wild landscape that would gradually be transformed into the Portland metropolitan area over the next 150 years.

In the early 1850s, close to a thousand households took up land in the future Portland region under the Donation Land Claim Act of 1850. This federal legislation rewarded early Oregon pioneers by allowing them to claim 320 acres (640 acres for a married couple). As census takers made their way from house to house across fresh-flowing streams and stump-filled fields in the spring of 1860, they recorded information that gives us snapshots of Portland's early landholders.

Two miles east of the Willamette, Timothy and Margaret Sullivan farmed 319 acres that spanned the gulch to which they gave their name. They were Irish born, but had reached Oregon the long way around via Australia, where they had married and had two children in the 1840s. They endured the long voyage to Oregon in 1850 and recorded their claim the following year.

Farther north, where higher land dropped to the Columbia Slough, was the Whitaker clan—Anthony from Ireland, Isabella from Scotland, a son born in Missouri, and two younger daughters born in Oregon. Henry McEntire, a laborer, and Susan Fitzgerald, an 11-year-old born in Missouri—maybe a servant, maybe a cousin, maybe a family friend—rounded out the household. Nearby, on land now occupied by Portland International Airport, were the Holtgrieves, Henry from Germany and Elizabeth from Iowa, with three-year-old Emma and infant Oceana (a name that hopefully did not burden her later in life).

Many households included single men as well as the core family—evidence that the frontier attracted the young, restless, and unemployed. The Tibbetts establishment in the future Brooklyn neighborhood included two farmhands, and Perry Prettyman's farm near Mount Tabor required three laborers to supplement family. The Wilcoxes at Hillsboro hired a farmhand from Ireland, but the Stotts in the future Beaverton made do with their teenaged sons.

Some of the early claimants were winners, and some were not. Many sold and moved on over the course of the 1850s. Some stuck, like Amos King, who arrived in Oregon in 1849 and sealed a deal for Daniel Lownsdale's tannery and a claim of 535 acres that ran from the modern Lovejoy Street south through what is now the King's Hill neighborhood. He built a spacious house just south of Burnside in 1856 and lived comfortably for the next 45 years. Not so fortunate was hot-tempered Danford Balch, whose farmstead was located along "Balch Creek" at what is now the Upshur Street entrance to Macleay Park. On November 18, 1858, authorities arrested him for the very public murder of an unwanted son-in-law at the Stark Street Ferry. He broke from Portland's flimsy jail and hid for weeks in the forest above his farm before he was recaptured and executed in 1859, leaving seven children at home as well as his estranged daughter.

Only in the nascent towns were there landowners who did not describe themselves as farmers. George Abernathy, who owned acres above Oregon City, was a merchant, but his son James has come down recorded as a farmer. In Portland itself, William Chapman was a lawyer. John Couch was a wharfinger or warehouse keeper, although much of his family money would come from increasing land values in Northwest Portland. Stephen Coffin was more blunt; he was a "townsite proprietor," a land speculator pure and simple.

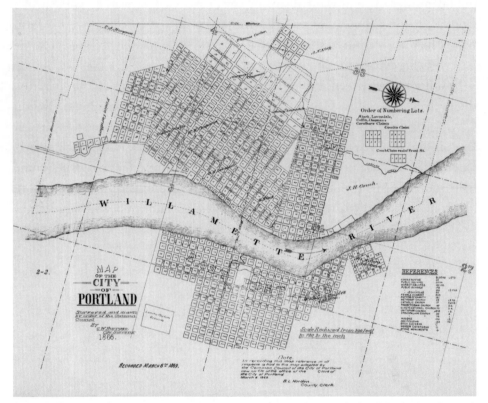

Map of Portland, 1866. By 1866, land speculators had extended the original plat of Portland to the north and south and across the river to lay out the beginnings of East Portland. Tanner Creek flows from the West Hills along the western edge of town and empties into the Willamette north of the wetlands that are now the upscale River District. (Portland City Archives)

Chapter 2
On the Edge of the West

Portlanders have always lived on the edge of the West. The "real West" of Zane Gray and Louis L'Amour begins closer to a hundred miles inland at The Dalles or Redmond, and stretches across another thousand miles of sagebrush, dry gulches, rocky mountains, and high plains. The Oregon pioneers of 1844 and 1845 hurried through this landscape, their covered wagons pointed toward the green vision of the Willamette Valley. The western interior is also the territory to which Portlanders returned their attention in the 1860s and 1870s to secure their fortunes. Portland's success story is a chronicle of valley dwellers who learned to tap the wealth of the dry country without leaving their drizzly metropolis.

After the California Gold Rush boom, new discoveries of gold in the interior of the Northwest gave Portland its second and most essential spurt of growth. The boom of 1848–49 and the benefits of victory over river-town rivals in 1850–51 had faded by the middle 1850s. A national depression compounded problems at the end of the decade. Portland in 1860 was still economically dependent on San Francisco, prospering when Californians wanted Oregon wheat and suffering when the demand slackened.

Mining strikes in Idaho, Montana, and the interior of the Columbia River Basin provided Portland a strong impetus for growth. A gold rush to Idaho's Clearwater River in August 1860 was as fortuitous for Portlanders as for the prospectors. During the next four years, miners fanned out from Idaho's Salmon River and Boise Basin, the Owyhee River on the present Oregon-Idaho border, Bannack City and Gold City in western Montana, and the Kootenay River just over the border in Canada. The old trading center of Walla Walla, Washington, and the new town of Lewiston, Idaho, were the final outfitters for the mines, but Portland was the supply base and jumping-off point during these frenetic boom years. More than 15,000 people passed upriver through Portland in 1861; 24,000 in 1862; and 22,000 in 1863. The *Oregonian* reported gleefully that "rents are up to an exorbitant figure, many houses contain two or more families, and the hotels and boardinghouses are crowded almost to overflowing. The town is full of people . . . buildings are going up . . . wharves stretching their proportions along the levees, and a general thrift and busy hum greet the ear."

Portland monopolized the growing business of the Pacific Northwest because of geography and because of the Oregon Steam Navigation Company (OSNC)—Oregon's first "millionaire-making machine" in the words of one early employee. The company's leading figure was John C. Ainsworth, a former Mississippi River steamboat captain who had been the first master of the Milwaukie steamship the *Lot Whitcomb*. He knew that navigation on the Columbia was interrupted by rapids at "the Cascades" and again by Celilo Falls at The Dalles. If Portland were to profit from the river, there needed to be something better than crude portages around both barriers. In 1860, Ainsworth formed the OSNC to unite the businesses that operated segments of the Columbia River route. The new corporation controlled improvements at both bottlenecks, operating a 6-mile railroad on the north bank of the Columbia to carry traffic around the rapids at what is now the town of Cascade Locks and a 14-mile road to bypass the long stretch of falls and rocks around The Dalles. OSNC investors Simeon Reed, Robert R. Thompson, William S. Ladd, and others who put up large chunks of capital learned the value of conservative management as they plowed back profits to expand and improve service. The OSNC operated steamers, wagon trains, stage lines, and connecting boats on the Snake River, Lake Pend Oreille, and the headwaters of the Missouri River, establishing a powerful transportation monopoly.

Few residents of eastern Oregon, eastern Washington, or Idaho had a kind word for the OSNC. They paid high charges on the cargo they imported and shipped out via the Columbia. Rumor had it that the company paid for a new steamer with the profits from a single trip upriver from Portland to the gold-mining country. Through the OSNC, pioneers and prospectors indirectly paid for the growth of Portland by generating the fortunes that Ladd, Ainsworth, Reed, and their colleagues invested in the city's factories, utilities, and real estate.

New settlers in Oregon's Willamette Valley heartland kept in touch with Portland by commerce along the river. Steamers reached upstream to Albany, Corvallis, and Harrisburg (nearly to Eugene) depending on the depth of water, picking up produce that farmers laboriously hauled to landings. Riverboats served Dayton, Lafayette, and McMinnville, which all grew up facing the

River traffic. In the late 1800s, Portland's waterfront teemed with high-masted grain and lumber schooners, oceanic steamers with routes to California and Asia, and smaller steamboats that carried freight and passengers up and down the Columbia. This view shows a coal ship unloading its cargo to power the city's riverfront factories and railroads. (Portland City Archives, A2004-022.2985)

saffron-colored Yamhill River. In 1870, six of Oregon's seven largest towns hugged the riverbanks. Seasonal floods reminded residents of the power of the natural environment. Portland's wharves were built in two levels—one for low water and one for high.

Those wharves, essential to Portland's economy, were private property on private land. Through much of the 1850s, the city had contended that the land east of Front Street was a "public levee" as in cities like St. Louis and New Orleans, and should be kept free of private buildings. Potential property owners, including the Lownsdale family, disagreed, arguing that their claims extended to the water. In 1861, Judge Matthew Deady found that the city had failed to consistently assert public ownership and decided for the Lownsdales. As historian Jewel Lansing points out, it took another half century before the city raised the funds to buy back control of sections of the riverbank.

The OSNC made Portland the true gateway to the Northwest, but the city would remain a second-class citizen in the commercial world as long as the latest news and mail arrived only twice a month by steamer from the Golden Gate. In 1860 the California Stage Company cut the time in half when it signed a contract to carry mail overland from Sacramento to Portland. Service began in September. The running time was seven days during the dry season, optimistically defined as running from April through December. Midwinter running time was 12 days, as drivers contended with hub-deep mud, landslides, and sudden snows in the Siskiyous. By 1866, when Portland's Henry Corbett took over the route, the time in good weather was down to five-and-a-half days. In the years before railroads began to creep south, the stage line was essential in connecting Jackson and Douglas counties to the rest of Oregon.

In 1864, the telegraph replaced the creaking and bouncing stagecoach as the conveyor of essential news. The California State Telegraph Company strung wires north from Sacramento and Maryville to Yreka in 1858. W. S. Ladd, S. G. Reed, H. W. Corbett, and A. L. Lovejoy incorporated the Oregon Telegraph Company in 1862 to make the connection. The Portland company's first load of wire sank in a shipwreck while en route from San Francisco, but the company ran its line through Aurora, Salem, Corvallis, Roseburg, and on to California in 1863. The first dispatch from San Francisco arrived in Portland on March 8, 1864, with news that had originated in New York just 20 hours earlier. The mayors of Portland, Oregon, and Portland, Maine, exchanged congratulatory messages. Other lines tied Portland to Seattle, Walla Walla, and Boise before the decade was out. The rate for sending 10 words to the East Coast was $7.50—enough to feed a Portland family for a week or educate a public school pupil for a year.

Rails followed the roads and wire. Railroad building south from Portland confirmed the city's dominance in Oregon. Rails supplemented and then replaced Willamette River steamers as the spread of agriculture made the river gradually more difficult to navigate. Cleared fields meant silt-laden runoff to clog the river. Logging meant more downed trees for heavy rains to wash into the river as hull-killing snags. In effect, railroads arrived just in time to save Portland's Willamette Valley trade.

Railroad building also shook the conservative Portland establishment by introducing them to Ben Holladay. An unscrupulous but highly successful businessman, Holladay had built the Overland Mail Company into the country's largest stage line in the 1860s. He had sold his company to Wells Fargo in 1868 and turned his attention to railroad building in the Pacific Northwest. Proper Portlanders were fascinated by his success and repelled by his style of life. They whispered that he populated his house with high-priced prostitutes, and they competed to find the right adjectives for him: *vulgar, low, haughty, dictatorial, dishonest,* and *immoral* were some of the favorites.

Holladay used the money from the sale of Overland Mail to plunge into a struggle between rival companies that wanted to build a Portland–California railroad on opposite sides of the Willamette. The west-side line was the Oregon Central Railway Company, backed by the Portland establishment of Reed, Corbett, and Ladd, who wanted to make sure that Willamette Valley trade poured directly into the city and added to the business of the OSNC. Holladay took them on by purchasing control of the east-side line, which he named the Oregon and California Railroad Company in 1869. At stake were not only freight and passengers, but also a federal land grant of 20 square miles for every mile of track. It would go to the first railroad that finished 20 miles of operational line. His enemies later claimed that Holladay spent $35,000 to bribe the state legislature to rescind a premature declaration in favor of the Oregon Central Railway. However, he also had the drive and money to finish the necessary track, win the grant, and buy out the defeated west-side line.

As the Oregon and California Railroad (eventually absorbed into the Southern Pacific system) pushed slowly southward, Holladay put together a tottering transportation empire in Portland. He owned docks, warehouses, and steamships. He monopolized the local transfer of passengers and freight. Expecting that an east bank railroad would shift the city's economic center across the river and that a growing city would require the lands of the east side, he built two hotels, grabbed a large chunk of waterfront, and laid out Holladay's Addition to East Portland in the present Lloyd Center area.

Portlanders tolerated Holladay's presence until 1874, when he came up nearly $500,000 short in interest payments on money borrowed from German investors. Eastern banker Henry Villard, a German-born newspaperman who was gaining a reputation as a shrewd businessman, investigated the viability of their investments for the German bondholders. In 1876, Villard bought out

Holladay and laid the foundation for his own railroad kingdom, completing the Oregon and California Railroad through Medford to California in 1883.

The growth of Willamette Valley farming was less spectacular than Idaho gold rushes and less exciting than Ben Holladay's full-throttle railroad career, but it was the most solid foundation for Portland's growth. Between 1860 and 1880, Oregon's acreage of improved farmland grew by 150 percent. Wheat production rose by 800 percent, and Portland merchants began to ship grain directly to Liverpool at the end of the 1860s. The frontier was changing fast. One of the shrewdest observers of the midcentury American West was Massachusetts newspaper editor Samuel Bowles. *Across the Continent*, published in 1865, offers a classic description of the Rockies and Pacific Coast; his account of Portland summed up the city's expanding economic base:

> Portland, by far the largest town in Oregon, stands sweetly on the banks of the Willamette . . . Ships and ocean steamers of highest class come readily hither; from it spreads out a wide navigation by steamboat of the Columbia and its branches, below and above; here centers a large and increasing trade, not only for the Willamette Valley, but for the mining regions of eastern Oregon and Idaho, Washington Territory on the north, and parts even of British Columbia.

Growing business demanded new architecture. The first downtown in the 1850s had been built in a long strip parallel to the river. After 1871, horse-car lines operated by the Portland Street Railway Company made First Street between Davis and Salmon the main business thoroughfare. Five horse-drawn rail cars covered a 1.5-mile route. By 1880, they carried six hundred passengers per day at 10 cents a head.

Property owners replaced flimsy wood buildings with an elegant city of cast iron. The typical new mercantile building was a two- or three-story brick or masonry shell with an elaborate façade of cast iron. Detailed pillars and pilasters, capitals, cornices, and medallions imitated carved stone and turned ordinary buildings into "commercial palaces." By the 1880s, nearly two hundred buildings sported cast-iron fronts. The twenty that remain have survived 19th-century floods and fires and 20th-century neglect. Most are now protected within the Yamhill and Skidmore-Old Town historic districts, designated by the city council in 1975 and recognized on the National Register of Historic Places.

The heart of this early downtown was the corner of First and Ankeny. The New Market building, built for Captain Alexander Ankeny in 1872, was

Northern Pacific Railroad celebration arch. Portlanders erected three ceremonial arches over First Avenue in 1883 and decorated many of the buildings along the street to celebrate the completion of the city's Northern Pacific Railroad link with the eastern United States. (Gholston Collection)

the hub of Portland for the next decade. A drive-through market took up the first floor; a theater lit by a hundred gas jets was on the second. Within a short walk were the Board of Trade, the telegraph office, and the docks of the Oregon Steam Navigation Company. This corner would also provide the site for the elegant fountain that Stephen Skidmore donated in 1888 to provide water for thirsty "men, horses, and dogs."

Much farther from the center was a three-story post office and a federal court building surmounted by a two-story cupola. When work on the "Pioneer Courthouse" started in 1869, and even when it was finished in 1875, Portlanders considered it far too distant from the bustling business center. Wits quipped that the city needed a pony express to carry mail back and forth from the riverfront, but the view from the cupola—for a number of years the best vantage point short of the West Hills—became part of the standard itinerary for visitors.

Portland's population grew as fast as its trade. The 2,800 residents of 1860 more than doubled by 1864. In the Pettygrove and Coffin eras, everyone who counted in Portland knew everyone else. By 1863, however, the city was big enough to need its first annual city directory, published by former mayor S. J. McCormick. The population continued to grow to 8,300 in 1870, and 17,600 by 1880.

These were the years when Portland far outdistanced its Oregon rivals. In the 1860s, places like Salem, Oregon City, or The Dalles could still hold

ambitions to catch up to or even pass Portland. By 1880, it was clear that the
state had *one* dominant city. Portland was larger than the next dozen towns
added together. The second-largest city in 1880, Astoria, counted only 2,803
people—just one-seventh of Portland's population. Salem, with 2,538 people,
was one-eighth as large. The Dalles, with 2,232, and Albany, with 1,867, were
even further behind.

Railroads and steamers made Portland a center for ideas as well as commerce. At the end of the 1870s, readers in the city and the greater Northwest
supported a score of periodicals ranging from daily newspapers to scientific
journals. Citizens dissatisfied with the weighty *Oregonian* could read the daily
Bee, *Standard*, or *Telegram*. The weekly *Sunday Mercury*, *Sunday Welcome*,
and *Sunday Call* (out of East Portland) supplemented the dailies. The *Pacific
Christian Advocate* carried news to northwestern Methodists, the monthly
Columbia Churchman to Episcopalians, and the weekly *Catholic Sentinel* to
Roman Catholics. There was a weekly *Willamette Farmer*, a monthly *Medical
Journal*, and a semi-monthly *Journal of Education*.

The magazine *West Shore* (1875–91) was the epitome of 19th-century
boosterism. Editor L. Samuel served up lavishly illustrated articles on the
progress and possibilities of Portland and the Pacific Northwest. Stories of
economic growth and pictures of new buildings and bridges had wide appeal
up and down the coast. The list of subscribers grew from 9,000 in 1880 to
37,500 in 1890 before overextension put the publication out of business.

The founder and editor of the weekly newspaper *New Northwest*
(1871–87) was Abigail Scott Duniway, who advocated for women's rights,
women's suffrage, "Eternal Liberty," and "Untrammeled Progression." The
masthead spelled out Duniway's philosophy: "A Journal for the People,
Devoted to the Interests of Humanity, Independent in Politics and Religion,
Alive to All Live Issues and Thoroughly Radical in Opposing and Exposing
the Wrongs of the Masses." Each weekly issue offered news on business and
cultural events, descriptions of prisons and asylums, reports on Duniway's
constant travels on the Western lecture circuit, and acerbic editorials against
mossbacked opponents of female emancipation and social progress. There
were sometimes stories by famous writers like Bret Harte and Mark Twain,
as well as the serialized fiction that served as frontier soap operas. Duniway
herself wrote 17 serialized novels during the paper's 16-year life. Behind the
melodrama in such stories as *Madge Morrison: The Molalla Maid and Matron*,
Ethel Graeme's Destiny, and other titles were lessons about the problems of
unloving and unequal marriages. Abigail Duniway certainly had one of the
most energetic minds in late 19th-century Portland and quite possibly the

brightest. The latter was something that *Oregonian* editor Harvey Scott, her curmudgeonly brother and political opponent, would never admit on the pages of his newspaper.

The Portland press served immigrants along with English-speaking residents. The *Deutsche Zeitung* after 1867 and the *Staats Zeitung* after 1877 kept the German language alive. New arrivals from Germany could put up at the Deutsches Gast Haus (also known as the New York Hotel, for English-speaking guests), call on the German Aid Society, and drink lager brewed by a man appropriately named George Bottler. By 1880, several thousand German Americans supported four German-language churches and occasional stage performances in German.

A significant portion of German immigrants were Jews, who began to arrive from San Francisco or directly from Bavaria and southern Germany in the late 1850s. The city's Jewish population grew from 135 in 1860 to 768 in 1880. Helping to finance each other's businesses and drawing on Western business networks, many entered the retail dry goods and clothing businesses and gained positions of respect among the largely Protestant business community. A growing number of more religiously conservative Polish Jews balanced Congregation Beth Israel by organizing Ahavai Shalom in 1869.

The growth of Portland's African American population from 16 to 147 during the 1860s was a more severe test of local tolerance than the immigration of easily assimilated German Jews. In 1867, the school district and the courts refused to enter the four children of Maryland-born William Brown in the all-white public schools. The *Oregonian* applauded the alternative— the appropriation of $800 for a segregated school that would enroll up to 25 black students between 1867 and 1872. But with the onset of a major national economic depression brought on by the Panic of 1873, the principle of segregation hardly seemed worth the cost, and African Americans quietly entered the regular schools.

African American population numbers were too small to make a major impression on the city, but the community developed its own institutions, such as the AME Zion church in 1862, and staged annual celebrations of the Emancipation Proclamation in the years after the Civil War. In 1869, the event took place on January 1. The public was invited to the county courthouse at 6:00 p.m. to hear poetry, vocal and instrumental music, and an oration by Bishop Ward of the African Methodist Episcopal Mission (William Brown was the presiding officer for the day). Perhaps because of such well-managed activities, Judge Matthew Deady was satisfied to report that the African American community was "moderately thrifty and well conducted."

In fact, Deady was pleased with almost everything about his city. Writing a profile of "Portland-on-Wallamet" for the first issue of San Francisco's *Overland Monthly*, he described it as a "solid and reliable town." It would never be the center of fashion, he explained, but the blue river and the sublime Monarch of the Mountains glistening above the dark forests 40 miles to the east were more than adequate compensation. Portland's good citizens, Deady told his readers, would "sleep sounder and live longer" than frantic San Franciscans. Oregon historian Francis Fuller Victor, who had lived in both California and Oregon, shared Deady's assessment. She thought the Portland of 1871 "a cheerful-looking town . . . with handsome public buildings and comfortable, home-like dwellings." The well-to-do could pass their time with pleasure drives on the macadamized road that ran up the west side of the Willamette to the Riverside Race Course. And, wrote Victor, on sunny afternoons the "youth, beauty, and fashion of Portland" strolled the public squares opposite the courthouse to the bright music of brass bands.

City government in those early years tried to keep Portland pleasant for its business and professional families. One ordinance prohibited fast riding and driving "at a furious pace" anywhere east of Fourth Street, and another banned horses and wagons from sidewalks. An early version of the Oregon bottle bill made it unlawful "to throw, deposit, or leave any glass bottles or other glass vessels in the streets." Residents were to pick up litter to the midline of the street in front of their premises. The city encouraged the growing of shade trees and spent a substantial $32,000 to buy the 40-acre nucleus for Washington Park in 1871.

One of the most important public services relied on private enterprise. The city's first privately financed water system used wooden pipes. Workers laboriously drilled 2.5-inch holes down the center of fir logs and fitted them together with wooden sleeves, leading water from Marquam Creek (yes, there was a creek where that tangle of freeway ramps now stands at the south end of downtown) a mile or so into town. There followed thirty years of hit-or-miss service. Private water companies tapped Balch Creek for "uphill" properties west of Fourth Street. They built reservoirs at Fifteenth and Alder, Fourth and Market, and Sixth and Lincoln. They installed steam pumps to tap the Willamette, especially at the imposing Palatine Hill Pumping Station, opened for action in 1884.

Portlanders who ventured off their front porches in the "suburbs" west of Sixth Street could find a less-sedate city if they knew where to look. Many theaters catered to the popular taste with "low grade minstrels and vulgar comedy." British visitor Wallis Nash in 1877 complained that *Othello* fell flat compared with the "half hour of screaming farce" that followed. Thousands of patrons crowded into more than two hundred saloons to drink, gamble, and try out Phelan's Patent Billiard Tables. The Oro Fino saloon and theater at Front and Stark advertised "the choicest qualities of wines and liquors, ales, port, and fine cigars." It belonged to James Lappeus, Portland's city marshal from 1859 to 1861 and chief of police from 1870 to 1877 and again from 1879 to 1883.

Law enforcement efforts expanded with the city. A part-time marshal was adequate to keep the peace at the start of the 1860s, but the city hired two deputies by mid-decade and established a formal police force in 1870. Six officers covered three beats north of Oak, between Oak and Yamhill, and south of Yamhill. Their biggest task was to run in drunks who threatened to tear up the town. With the police chief counted among their number, saloon owners and gamblers had less trouble than might have been expected: Portland's police were not energetic about enforcing liquor and gambling laws. Saloon keeper Edward Chambreau later recalled of this era: "The first thing I did when I took charge of the 'Hell Hole' [meaning his saloon] was to *fix* the policeman on my beat." Economic growth brought more opportunities for creative crime, as the Police Commission noted in 1874:

> The number of arrests for 1873 are about double the number of any year prior to 1871 . . . The perpetrators of housebreaking and high-way robbery find this too hazardous to pursue, and have changed their occupations and found encouragement in a higher role . . . A number of these dangerous characters are to be seen daily about our docks and custom house, placed side by side with many honest laborers, ready always to extend the hand of friendship to the crews of newly arrived vessels, and to tender their services to show them "the sights about town"—through the "dives" where these charac-ters and female "pals" do dwell. The sailor is easily imposed upon generally, and becomes an easy victim. His gold is soon gone . . . and he is unable to tell by whom or how, for when it is done he is usually intoxicated, and thus the thieves escape detection and arrest. The great increase of our commerce has opened a wide field for the operations of these persons.

Portland's decision makers thought that jackrolled sailors were a small price to pay for commercial expansion. They also knew that the next necessary step was a direct transcontinental railroad connection. Hopes rose in 1870 when the Northern Pacific Railway decided to build down the Columbia and engaged in a stock swap that made the Oregon Steam Navigation Company a wholly owned subsidiary. But hopes fell with the financial crash of 1873, which drove the Northern Pacific into bankruptcy, brought the OSNC back to its original owners, and halted construction on the Northern Pacific and other railroads for five years.

Henry Villard filled the vacuum. He controlled Ben Holladay's system of Willamette Valley railroads after 1876. In 1879 he bought out the OSNC and formed a new Oregon Railway and Navigation Company, which included his entire Oregon rail and steamship operations. Villard's greatest coup came in 1881. Raising $8 million from fifty capitalists, he gained control of the Northern Pacific and made himself the transportation king of the Northwest. While Portland businessmen lobbied the federal government to dredge the bar at the mouth of the Columbia, Villard tried to develop transportation links to the east. The main line of the Northern Pacific was complete at the end of the summer of 1883. A corporate peace treaty had already given the Union Pacific access to Portland over Northern Pacific tracks, and the Northern Pacific reciprocal use of Union tracks into Utah. When a Union Pacific branch reached the Northern Pacific tracks at Huntington, Oregon, in December 1884, Portland gained the advantage of service by two transcontinental railroads.

Henry Villard celebrated completion of the Northern Pacific by hauling four trainloads of dignitaries from the East and bringing another train from San Francisco and Portland to the golden-spike ceremony at Deer Lodge, Montana. The eight VIPs on the West Coast special could wander through four Pullman cars, two dining cars, and two commissary cars. A potpourri of diplomats, New York bankers, German financiers, congressmen, and governors watched the driving of the golden spike (actually ordinary steel) late in the afternoon of September 8, 1883. The line had opened to traffic in August, but trains had moved on a bypass, leaving a half-mile gap in the main line to be officially closed in front of former president Ulysses S. Grant and hundreds of Crow Indians in full regalia at the Deer Lodge shindig. It was the first step in a systematic publicity campaign to bring investment and settlers to the High Plains and Inland Empire through Northern Pacific agents in Liverpool, Hamburg, New York, Boston, Omaha, and Portland.

Villard, Grant, and the rest of the party steamed into East Portland several hours behind schedule, on the evening of September 10. The grand parade was postponed until the next day, but thousands of enthusiastic Portlanders still turned out along First Street to welcome the train. On the 11th, country people packed the ferries and crowded the roads into town. Restaurants served the throngs on double shifts at double time. The parade looped south on Fourth to Hall, gathered momentum back up Third to Burnside, and turned back on First to the Mechanics Pavilion, where the Keller Auditorium now resides. Unlucky businessmen and their wives had to sit through the obligatory speeches, while average Portlanders got to enjoy the rest of the informal holiday in the bright sunshine. Board of Trade President Donald Macleay expressed the reason for the excitement in one sentence: "We are now connected with the rest of the world."

East side. In 1895, after consolidation with Portland, the east side of the Willamette was a mix of waterfront businesses, scattered housing, farms, and a few remaining chunks of uncleared land. This view looks northeast across the Morrison Bridge, with Sullivan's Gulch and the Alameda Ridge visible on the left side of the image. (Portland City Archives, A2004-002.956)

Chapter 3
Growing Up and Settling Down

Portland was still a small community at the time of its railroad revolution. With only 17,000 residents on the west side of the Willamette and a few hundred more scattered among the fir-covered ravines and knolls of the east side, Portland in 1880 was approximately the same size as The Dalles or Pendleton today. In an 1880 compendium entitled *The Social Statistics of Cities*, the Census Bureau reported that "the growth of Portland has been moderately steady." The tone of Portland life appeared to federal officials to be that of a country town rather than a bustling city. "The population is American, with a large mixture of Europeans and Mongolians [Chinese]. Business is in the hands of men from the eastern and middle states, Great Britain, and Germany. Education is guided by Americans from New England and the northern states. The New England element has had a marked influence throughout."

Twenty years later, Portland was a metropolis. Transcontinental railroad links facilitated immigration, boosted business, and helped to more than quintuple Portland's population to 90,000 in 1900. Portland in its first generation had been the isolated center for an "island" of settlement along the Willamette and Columbia. During the 1880s and 1890s, the Northern Pacific and Union Pacific railways joined it to the rest of the nation.

Portland was a diversified city at the time it made its transcontinental rail connection. About a thousand workers in small factories manufactured iron products and processed agricultural goods for customers in the Northwest and produced lumber, furniture, doors, and other building materials for buyers up and down the West Coast. The city directories of the early 1880s listed about a hundred merchants under the categories of dry goods wholesaler, liquor dealer, grain dealer, commission merchant, grocery wholesaler, and hardware dealer. The city's middle class included lawyers, bank tellers, clerks, retailers, and owners of small industrial firms. A larger working class supplied the muscle power for transportation and construction work.

Residents in 1880 had a small town's "self-help" approach to public services. They bought water and coal gas for lighting from private companies. The city paid the bills for a variety of unsatisfactory street pavements—stone blocks, chunks of wood set grain-end up, gravel, and planks, but adjacent property owners were required to sweep or scrape the pavements every Friday afternoon. Householders had to haul their own garbage and street sweepings to the outskirts of town. Protection from serious fires, such as those the city had suffered in 1872 and 1873, was still in the hands of five volunteer engine companies and a hook and ladder company. A paid fire chief and two assistants supervised four hundred volunteers. The city owned a police station (with jail) and several firehouses, but the mayor, treasurer, and city attorney had so little to do that the city didn't even provide them office space.

The informal approach to public services and government ended with the arrival of the transcontinental railroad. By the end of the 1890s the city government had increased its responsibilities to include parks, street lighting, sewers, water, and public health. The police department had grown, and firefighters were converted to full-time employees.

Nothing changed the city more than the construction of bridges across the Willamette. The first was the Morrison Bridge, the largest span west of the Mississippi when the Willamette Iron Bridge Company finished it in April 1887. By contributing to east-side development, it also marked a basic change in the shape of the city. A railroad bridge (Steel Bridge) followed in 1888; it opened to wagons and streetcars a year later. Private investors built a rickety wooden Madison Street Bridge in 1891 and sold it to the city a year later. The city also erected the more expensive Burnside Bridge in 1894. The first three bridges have been replaced twice and the Burnside Bridge is in its second incarnation. The bridges quickly replaced the Stark Street and Albina ferries, but not the Sellwood steam ferry that continued to operate three miles upriver.

Portlanders could reasonably expect to walk around a town of 17,000, but they needed the help of mechanically powered streetcars in a city of 90,000. Between 1885 and 1895 the city council granted dozens of franchises allowing private companies to build and operate street railways on public rights-of-way. Small steam engines on the first east-side line hauled passengers across the Morrison Bridge to the new neighborhoods of Sunnyside and Mount Tabor. The first electrified trolley crossed the Steel Bridge to Williams Avenue in 1889. A year later, the Portland Directory noted that electric trolleys would soon "do away entirely with the tedious and obsolete horse car."

Morrison Bridge. William Beck, active for years in trying to bridge the Willamette, was reported to have "cried like a child" when the impressive Morrison Bridge opened in 1887. A drawbridge span had eliminated objections from people concerned about river navigation. Since then, 19 different structures have been built to span the river—for railroads, streetcars, automobiles, bicycles, and pedestrians—with a further two in the planning stage as of 2011. (Gholston Collection)

Dozens of electrified routes quickly proved the prediction, with 128 miles of trolley track by 1900. Streetcar service was especially good northward from the Steel Bridge along Albina, Williams, and Union (now Martin Luther King Jr. Boulevard) and directly east from the other bridges along Glisan, Belmont, Hawthorne, Clinton, and Gladstone. On the west side, where trolleys had a difficult time along the steep slopes, a cable car ran up an inclined plane that rose southward from Jefferson Street to Portland Heights in 1889.

The booming city required safe and abundant water for household use, industry, firefighting, and street cleaning (remember all those horses hitched to wagons and carriages). Water from the increasingly polluted Willamette was no good for a city that aspired to be another San Francisco—or to at least keep ahead of Seattle. In 1885 the legislature authorized the city to issue bonds and "to construct or purchase, keep, conduct, and maintain water works . . . to furnish the City and its inhabitants thereof with an abundance of good, pure, and wholesome water." The first result was a Water Committee of leading businessmen. Henry Failing was chair, and members included Henry Corbett, William S. Ladd, Simeon G. Reed, and Cicero S. Lewis. These movers and shakers studied, considered financial obligations, and decided that the Bull Run River on the northwest slope of Mount Hood was the best source of pure water. The system that sent its first water through Portland taps and hydrants on January 2, 1895, used 33-inch and 42-inch iron pipes to bring water 40 miles from the mountain and deliver it to Reservoir 1 on Mount

Perkins Hotel. R.S. Perkins used a fortune made in the cattle business to build a hotel in 1891 at Southwest Fifth and Washington, where he commemorated the source of his wealth with a large gilded cow in a corner tower (the building was demolished in 1962 and the cow resides in the Oregon Historical Society warehouse). Portland's connection with the cattle business would grow in the early twentieth century, when Swift and Company built a large stockyard and packing plant in North Portland and helped to create the adjacent Kenton neighborhood to house its workers. (Gholston Collection)

Tabor. From there it flowed to Mount Tabor Reservoir 2 at Sixtieth and Division (decommissioned in the 1970s) and under the river near Ross Island to Reservoirs 3 and 4 in Washington Park. Engineers used gravity to distribute the water when they could, and pumps and standpipes when they had to (in North Portland, for example).

Pure and abundant water was one of Portland's selling points as it competed for new investment with other Western cities. Water was also a marketing tool for new subdivisions; locals noticed that the straight conduit westward from Mount Tabor ran along Division Street and past William Ladd's new neighborhood of Ladd's Addition—a pleasant coincidence. But perhaps most important, a clean, reliable water supply made Portland one of the healthiest cities in the country in 1900.

Portlanders were also growing accustomed to streets being torn up and rebuilt to accommodate other pipes. They wanted drinking water in their homes but they didn't want rainwater flooding their streets, so workers channeled one natural stream after another through underground sewers, including

Tanner Creek and Balch Creek on the west side, streams that drained off Alameda Ridge, and watercourses that flowed and wound through low spots in southeast neighborhoods. Those with an eye for architectural styles can spot the drier blocks that attracted early builders and the wetter blocks that remained undeveloped until drainage was adequate. An example is the slough that crossed Southeast Grand around Oak and Pine and curved southeast for several blocks between Sixth and Seventh. The buildings on those blocks date from the 1910s or later, as compared to 19th-century buildings elsewhere in the Grand Avenue Historic District.

Bridges, streetcars, and Bull Run water were key to successful suburbanization east of the Willamette. East Portland and Albina originated as Portland's Jersey City and Hoboken, secondary industrial centers built around docks, sawmills, flour mills, and railroad yards. East Portland—stretching from the present Northeast Halsey to Southeast Holgate streets—was platted in 1861 and incorporated in 1870. Albina was laid out in 1873 and incorporated in 1887: the town was run by the Oregon Railroad and Navigation Company, whose riverfront shops had hundreds of workers, and one of the employees, D. M. McLaughlin, served as mayor from 1888 to 1891.

The east-side boom arrived with the Morrison Bridge. Speculators rushed to take advantage of improved transportation by laying out middle-class subdivisions on higher land set back from the rowdy waterfront. Irvington dates from 1887; Sunnyside and Central Albina (Boise) from 1888; and Woodlawn, Kenilworth, Woodstock, and Tabor Heights from 1889. Portlanders continued to pin high hopes on real estate in the early 1890s, adding Ladd's Addition, Brooklyn, Richmond, Arbor Lodge, University Park, and Piedmont. Every developer issued special maps and colored brochures promising fine residential neighborhoods. *Piedmont, The Emerald, Portland's Evergreen Suburb, Devoted Exclusively to Dwellings—A Place of Homes* was typical. Developer Edward Quackenbush assured potential customers that "no dwelling can be built at a cost of less than $2,000. Thus the surroundings are secure." Not to be outdone, a publicist for Ladd's Addition wrote in the *Oregonian Souvenir* (1892) that Mr. Ladd "has not only made every preparation to pave all the streets . . . at his own expense, but he has provided for supplying the residents of this tract with gas and electric lights, he has arranged for a splendid system of sewerage and drainage . . . He will lay sidewalks fronting on every block and he will have a perfect water system that will insure residents of an ample supply of the purest water for domestic purposes."

Sellwood was a "steamboat suburb" before the streetcar arrived. *Oregonian* publisher Henry Pittock headed the consortium that bought 321 acres originally developed as a commercial nursery and orchard by Oregon Trail pioneer Henderson Luelling. The community had five hundred residents by 1885, served by a ferry across the Willamette and by steam launch service into the city. The addition of streetcars in 1892 helped the population boom to 1,800 by the next year, when Sellwood was annexed to Portland.

In the decades before formal zoning codes, developers and residents used private deed restrictions to protect neighborhood character. Elizabeth Irving made sure to prohibit liquor manufacturing or sales in Irvington. Advertising copy claimed that William Ladd's "well-known aversion to the liquor traffic has led him to make provisions for excluding saloons from this tract [Ladd's Addition] for all time. He will allow no liquor to be sold on the property, a reservation which insures residents here of the freedom from a great annoyance which has baffled the efforts of many of the residents of Portland to remedy." The developers of Colonial Heights required a minimum house value of $5,500 and a 25-foot setback from the street for the blocks between Southeast Clay and Harrison (but only $3,500 and a 20-foot setback between Clay and Hawthorne). People who bought lots in Alameda accepted prohibitions on commercial uses, on board fences, and on selling or renting to persons of African or Asian descent. Common in other cities as well as Portland, such racially restrictive covenants remained an important tool for discrimination until the U.S. Supreme Court declared them unenforceable in 1948.

Whether the neighborhood was upscale or working class, its streets were usually made of dirt and gravel. In the summer, water wagons rumbled past, sprinkling streets to quell the dust, but delivery vans and carts still kicked up clouds of grime. November storms turned streets into seas of mud. Despite these drawbacks, streets in the days before automobiles were as much social spaces as transportation arteries. Householders chatted with their neighbors. Peddlers and scissor-grinders made their way from house to house. Sometimes there was even a band of roving musicians, who would tote their brass instruments through east-side neighborhoods and strike up German oompah melodies in the hope of cadging pennies and nickels from the neighborhood residents.

Wood smoke threw a pall over the city during the winter. Each fall, homeowners bought loads of logs, which were dumped on parking strips to wait for a horse-drawn wood saw to come past and cut them into stove lengths. Sometimes hobos would earn a meal by hauling the lengths to the woodshed behind people's kitchens. Piles of sawdust along the street served as sandboxes for kids. In Lucille MacDonald's neighborhood (where Lloyd Center now stands), the more prosperous households hired German and Russian immigrant women from Albina to help with the endless stream of laundry.

Skidmore Fountain. Funded in part by the estate of businessman and philanthropist Stephen Skidmore, the fountain was intended for the relief of "horses, men, and dogs." When it was dedicated in 1888, it stood among the warehouses and commercial buildings that were the heart of Portland's first business district. (Gholston Collection)

In spring, everyone pitched in to carry furniture outside into the fresh air. Children carefully pulled all the carpet tacks and helped to drag carpeting and mats to the backyard, where dad could beat out the soot and dust.

One result of the rapid economic and population growth brought by the railroad was the consolidation of the three separate cities into a single Portland. The 1890 census reported a disappointing population total for the west-side city. Worried that upstart Seattle was gaining on Portland, the Portland Chamber of Commerce began to push for a merger with East Portland and Albina. East-siders would benefit from the removal of bridge and ferry tolls, while businessmen would be able to impress outside investors with a higher population count. Consolidation passed handily in all three cities in a general referendum in 1891, instantly boosting the city's size and keeping it well ahead of Seattle and Tacoma into the 20th century. The land area within Portland city limits jumped from 7 square miles to 26, and 10,000 East Portlanders and more than 5,000 Albinians were added to the population rolls. Two years later the city grew another 50 percent in size by annexing chunks of the southwest hills, Sellwood, and subdivisions east of Twenty-Fourth Avenue. In 1880, when it had only 3,000 residents, the east side had been a neglected and scruffy fringe. Twenty years later, the 32,000 east-siders were an essential part of the city.

Chinatown. Portland's early Chinese residents spread through much of downtown between the 1860s and the early 1900s, but the early core of "Chinatown" was the blocks lying between Front, Second, Washington, and Jefferson. By the 1920s, "New Chinatown" had developed north of Burnside. In most cases, the Chinese appropriated existing buildings and adapted them with balconies, signs, and decorations. (Gholston Collection)

The Census Bureau's brief summary of Portland's population mix in 1880—American, with a large mixture of Europeans and Asians—was a preview of the segmented city that emerged by the turn of the century. The Willamette bridges and streetcar lines not only allowed local builders to put up thousands of new homes on previously inaccessible land, but also made it feasible for the city's residents to sort themselves by race, nationality, and income. The process created a neighborhood pattern somewhat like an elongated archery target. Downtown was the bull's-eye, surrounded by a ring of neighborhoods for immigrants and unskilled workers. Farther out was a second ring of middle- and upper-class neighborhoods, where more established or successful families lived.

Portland was, in fact, an immigrant city by the end of the century. The 1880s ushered in a thirty-year surge of European immigration to the United States, with new waves of immigrants from Italy, Greece, Hungary, Poland, and Russia joining the already-established streams from Germany, Ireland, and the Scandinavian countries. Portland never welcomed the volume of newcomers that landed in New York or clambered off trains in Chicago, but nevertheless, by 1900, 58 percent of its residents—52,000 out of 90,000—had either been born outside the United States or were the children of immigrants.

Portland's Chinatown in 1890 was second in size only to San Francisco's. The Chinese came to Oregon originally to construct railroads, but as those jobs dried up, more and more settled permanently in Portland. The city's Chinese population grew from 1,700 in 1880 to 4,400 in 1890 and 7,800 in 1900. Their numbers included refugees from less tolerant Seattle and Tacoma, which drove out their Chinese residents in 1885 and 1886. The center for Portland's Chinese neighborhood was Second and Alder. Most observers agreed that the district stretched from Ash or Pine to Market between the river and Third. Portland's standard brick and cast-iron buildings were transformed with wrought-iron balconies, paper lanterns, and brightly colored signs for Chinese food stores. The Chinese operated more than a hundred businesses by the late 1880s, but most were laborers, dishwashers, cooks, and laundrymen. Hundreds commuted seasonally to farms, lumber camps, and salmon-packing plants on the Columbia River.

Japanese immigrants began to replace Chinese after the United States imposed stringent limitations on Chinese immigration in 1882. By the end of the 1890s, about 1,200 newly arrived Japanese worked on railroad crews, with Portland as their home base. Early in the new century they would

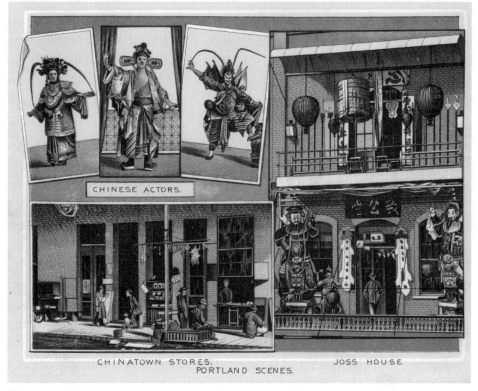

Chinatown scenes. Popular magazines often played up the exotic character of Chinese neighborhoods in cities like Seattle and Portland. (Gholston Collection)

turn to farming in the Portland area and to operating small stores, rooming houses, and affordable hotels in the blocks between Burnside Street and the new Union Station. What Portlanders several generations later called Old Town was sometimes called Nihonmachi or Japantown, but it was also one of the city's most diverse neighborhoods, with Chinese, Japanese, and Greek immigrants mingling with single male workers of all backgrounds and ethnicities.

A growing mix of European immigrants was simultaneously filling industrial neighborhoods on both sides of downtown. To the south, the blocks near Lownsdale Square held an assortment of saloons, labor exchanges, and cheap lodgings that blended imperceptibly into the European immigrant community of South Portland. South Portland's location between downtown and the manufacturing district of Fulton (Johns Landing) made it an entry point for unskilled workers new to the English language, particularly Italians and Jews from Russia and Eastern Europe.

Turn-of-the-20th-century Portland counted several other immigrant neighborhoods, although only fragments survive now. North of Burnside and west of Tenth were many Germans and Scandinavians living in "middle-class cottages, mostly unpretentious, but comfortable and occasionally showing signs of ambition" in the mildly condescending words of Harvey Scott. Most of that neighborhood was rebuilt as warehouses in the early 20th century and, of course, gentrified as the Pearl District by the 21st century, but several of its churches and missions still stand west of I-405. Irish and then Croatians clustered around northwest Nineteenth and Savier, in the Slabtown district close to sawmills, factories, and rail yards. St. Patrick's Church, built in 1891, served the two communities in succession.

Across the river, other Scandinavian immigrants and their children lived in Albina, with the working men near the railroads below the bluff and families on higher land around Williams and Union avenues. German-Russian immigrants — the descendants of Germans who had settled in Russian lands along the Volga in the 1700s — clustered near the present Irving Park, while Polish immigrants had begun to settle around Interstate and Failing, where St. Stanislaus Church would open in 1909. Over the decades, many of the area's churches would pass from one ethnic group to another. The Free Evangelical Brethren German Church (1904) on Northeast Mallory Avenue gained an onion dome and became St. Nicholas Russian-Greek Orthodox in 1930 and then passed to an African American congregation. The Norsk-Dansk Methodist Episcopal Kirke became First A.M.E. Zion Church, with a new cornerstone dated 1968 adjacent to the original dated 1909.

St. Patrick's Church. Built in 1891, St. Patrick's Church is now in the shadow of freeway ramps. When it opened, it was at the heart of the immigrant Slabtown neighborhood, named because its residents often heated their homes with the discarded slabwood from riverside sawmills. (Oregon Historical Society, Neg 36802)

The 1900 census gives a snapshot of Portland's immigrant population. Chinese were the largest contingent of foreign-born residents, with a count of 6,943. Next were Germans at 4,469, Britons at 2,686, and, not surprisingly, Canadians at 2,201. Japan, Ireland, and Sweden had each supplied more than 1,000 Portlanders. Russia was close behind at 984, followed by Norway with 850 and Italy with 631. Over the next decade, the totals would increase for every group but the Chinese. Compared to eastern cities like Boston, Buffalo, or Baltimore, Portland stood out for its Asian immigrants and for the continued dominance of newcomers from Europe's northwestern nations.

Underscoring the division between newly arrived immigrants and established Portlanders was the social distinction between unattached men and family households. Through the 1880s and 1890s, there were three males to every two females in the city. The Chinese, almost all of whom had arrived as single men, accounted for about half of the excess of 16,000 men at the end of the 19th century. Many others were European immigrants who came with the idea of making money and returning home to marry or, conversely, to establish themselves financially before sending for their family.

It was often all too easy to find men without families. All one had to do was to follow the loud music and the smell of stale beer to the riverfront blocks and downtown wards from Everett Street south to Jackson. The district included Chinatown, with its gambling halls, and a growing skid road around Burnside Street. The onset of cold weather brought several thousand seasonal farm, timber, and railroad workers to winter in the city's rooming houses, cheap hotels, and the back rooms of saloons.

Portland's well-justified reputation as a wide-open town was an important factor in pushing the respectable middle class into the new neighborhoods east of the river and the elite toward higher ground on the west. The increasing segregation of single men in a downtown district that met their needs and took their money also provided a prime target for moral reformers. The ensuing battles for temperance and clean living represented efforts to impose the standards of the native-born middle class and to demonstrate that Victorian family values had triumphed over the raw frontier.

The Chinese were the most obvious target for a police chief or mayor who wanted to prove his moral superiority. An 1851 ordinance against gambling had gone virtually unenforced until William Watkinds took office as police chief in 1883. Ignoring the thousands of white gamblers sitting down every night to faro and poker in Portland saloons, he systematically raided the fan-tan dens along Second Avenue and made nearly five hundred arrests in the course of the year. His patrolmen also brought in several dozen Chinese women on charges of prostitution, continuing the pattern of racially selective enforcement of the city's 1871 anti-prostitution law. Watkinds's immediate predecessor, James Lappeus, had been more concerned about Ordinance 2073, which prohibited smoking, buying, or possessing opium. As he explained in his 1879 annual report:

> Another evil, and a rapidly growing one, is the habit of opium smoking, which is ruining the health and destroying the minds of many of our young men and girls. There are a number of these dens, kept principally by Chinese, where men and women . . . congregate and indulge in this vile and filthy habit, and sleep off their stupor. Some of the females who frequent these places are married and have families, and young girls of the most respectable class of society. Could their names be published society would stand amazed . . . Some more stringent and severe measures should be taken to break up these dens of infamy.

Although Lappeus believed that several hundred white Portlanders puffed the opium pipe, their more common downfall was whiskey. In the spring of 1883, the city council adopted a prohibitive annual license fee of $500 for each of the city's 162 barrooms and saloons. Both temperance advocates and liquor interests focused their attention on the 1883 council election, which would determine if the high license fee would be sustained or repealed. The *Oregonian* and the Women's Christian Temperance Union saw the election as a contest between the "immoral, vicious, and disorderly classes" and the "decent part of the community." Local politicians saw only another power play in which temperance was a screen for maneuvering by political factions. Leaders of both parties quietly stacked the nominations with candidates who favored business as usual, and Portland awoke after the election to find two saloon operators ensconced in its governing body.

A decade later, the Portland Ministerial Association tried an even more direct approach to fight the liquor trade. It researched and published the names of landlords of more than two hundred drinking joints that operated illegally or after hours. Harry Perkins, a migratory laborer, described the Tenderloin between First, Seventh, Burnside, and Glisan in 1898, where there were "blocks on blocks given up to prostitution, gambling, saloons, and every variety of dive the world holds." A larger proportion of leading businessmen appeared on the list of property owners who profited from Demon Rum. Despite public embarrassment, there were enough members of the upper crust on the list that most owners decided to ride out the fuss without evicting their disreputable tenants.

The general lack of enthusiasm for temperance campaigns shows one way in which Portland's "other half" could defend its interests against middle-class strictures. Portland in the 1880s and 1890s was a city where political bosses mediated between working-class voters and the business elite. Each of the city's wards, of which there were eight after the consolidation of 1891 and ten by 1901, elected two members to the city council. The mayor had relatively little authority and, after 1885, shared executive powers with a separate Board of Police Commissioners. The police commissioners formed a corrupt alliance with the political machine. Mayor William Mason complained in the early 1890s about his inability to force tough law enforcement: "We lack the power to enforce the laws . . . Our police perambulate the streets day and night and we hear of no arrests for violations." Mason's fear that the police were "the protectors, the sharers in the spoils" of a corrupt system was certainly correct in the North End, where entrepreneur and future U.S. Senator Jonathan Bourne was the political boss who called the shots.

PORTLAND, OREGON, AND ITS SURROUNDINGS, 1889.
ISSUED BY THE OREGON IMMIGRATION BOARD.

1889 Birds-eye view. Portland in 1889 was poised for economic takeoff. Shown are the cutover hills behind the city center, the first streets of Portland Heights and double-wide blocks of Nob Hill, the original Morrison Bridge and the first Steel Bridge, and the concentration of industry along the waterfront. The smokestack for the Union Pacific shops in lower Albina still stands. (Oregon Historical Society, Neg 23627)

Although bosses claimed to look after working-class needs, labor unions offered a better long-term option. Efforts to organize Portland's skilled workingmen dated to the 1870s, but one of the first major events in local union history was a mass meeting in 1880 at which an organizer for the Knights of Labor addressed a crowd of 4,000. The following year brought the organization of several craft unions such as Local 50 of the Brotherhood of Carpenters and Joiners. When AFL President Samuel Gompers visited Portland in the late 1880s, the city's Federated Trades Assembly had 15 unions representing 400 members. The early union movement came to a climax in 1890, when Portlanders participated in a national drive for the eight-hour day in the building trades. Carpenters, painters, plumbers, and trimmers who participated in a strike and lockout ended with half a victory by agreeing to an eight-hour day but with proportionately reduced wages. In the mid-1890s, as the United States plunged into its deepest depression of the century after the Panic of 1893, Portland unionists struggled, though with limited success, to hold the gains of the previous years.

In the depths of the same depression, hundreds of other Portlanders marched behind the banner of the United States Industrial Army. "Coxey's Army," as it was called, was the plan of Ohioan Jacob Coxey to bring thousands of unemployed Americans from all over the country to a grand rally in Washington, D.C., where they would petition the federal government for work relief. In April 1894, recruiters for Portland's "commonweal companies" set up tables on the sidewalks of the North End and directed several hundred enlistees to a camp at the mouth of Sullivan's Gulch. Attacked by the press as "herds of vagrants" and lazy tramps, and denied food by the Board of Charities, the army walked the dozen miles to Troutdale, where, on April 27, they seized an Oregon Railway and Navigation Company train. Their intention was to head east, picking up recruits along the way and depending on help from sympathetic railroad workers. They got as far as Arlington (with a festive stop at The Dalles) before a detachment of cavalry from Walla Walla rescued the property of Portland's most powerful investors and arrested the train's hijackers. Federal judge C. B. Bellinger reprimanded and released the 439 prisoners. A crowd of sympathizers milled angrily around the Oregonian Building for several hours but dispersed without convincing editor Harvey Scott that the unemployed needed jobs rather than contempt.

Portlanders from overseas had to turn to each other to build their communities. Churches, neighborhoods, and benevolent societies all helped new Americans make their place in the growing city. People at the bottom of the economic pyramid—often these same immigrants and their children—also organized through trade unions and ward politics to protect their interests and battle for a share of the benefits of growth. Portlanders at the top had no such problems. They ran the city, and they assumed that to do so was their privilege and responsibility. The *Oregonian's Handbook of the Pacific Northwest*, a regional guide published in 1894, drew a clear-cut line between "progressive, intelligent, and cultured" citizens and "the debasing influence of foreign paupers." Harvey Scott, who was confident that he spoke for the better sort, was scornful of those who needed help in ascending to the heights of the "first-class" citizen. From the pages of the *Oregonian* he growled against public high schools, women's suffrage, and the reformers of the Populist Party. He thought that the Chinese were "not very desirable people" but worth tolerating because their services in housework, wood-cutting, laundries, and construction gangs allowed for work of a more "rewarding kind for the American."

Portland's "Americans," particularly the fortunate few, were directly affected by the emergence of large corporations that marked a change in the national economy. After 1880, the Portland City Directory found it impossible to continue listing every new building and every incorporation for the past year. The general-purpose merchant of Portland's pioneer decade was gradually replaced by firms that specialized in fruit or hardware or men's furnishings. There was one category of insurance broker in 1880 and a dozen categories by 1900. Before the Northern Pacific Railroad arrived, the typical factory was a small shop where the owner knew his six or seven employees. Although Portland still had no giant factories on the scale of those in Pittsburgh or Chicago at the turn of the 20th century, its lumber mills averaged a hundred workers in 1900 and a hundred and fifty by 1905. Its furniture factories, sash and door makers, and packing houses averaged thirty or forty hands.

Factory owners could show their wares and discover new ideas at the Portland Mechanics Fair, held every September from 1880 through 1888 in the Pavilion on the future site of the City Auditorium. The success of the Mechanics Fair paved the way for the North Pacific Industrial Exposition. A great success until the depression of 1893, the Industrial Exposition occupied a vast new structure covering two full blocks at Nineteenth and Washington and included a music hall with seating for five thousand. Promoters claimed it was the largest building on the Pacific coast.

The arrival of big manufacturing and specialized commerce required new methods to maintain common goals within the business community. The Portland Chamber of Commerce organized in 1890 and the Manufacturers Association in 1895. Flamboyant real estate developer William Killingsworth helped to create a new Board of Trade in 1899 to attract men of "push and progress" in both commerce and the professions. Social clubs were an equally important way for the elite to set themselves apart. The Commercial Club, founded in 1893, devoted itself to entertainment, socializing, and business promotion. The Arlington Club incorporated in 1881. It met first in J. C. Ainsworth's old house, then in its own building at Park and Alder, and eventually in its current building after 1910. It was the city's most exclusive refuge for white businessmen with big bank accounts. As historian E. Kimbark MacColl pointed out in *The Shaping of a City*, "the large banks, the utilities, the railroads, and Oregon's United States Senators were especially well represented within the Arlington Club's membership. During the 1890s the club could normally count at least four or five of its members serving in a session of the Oregon Legislature. The direct political influence of the club reached its peak around 1900 with two successive mayors who were members."

In an increasingly segmented city, the economic upper class was eager not only to control important decisions but also to create a life apart from the ordinary folk. The *Portland Blue Book* of 1890, published out of San Francisco, and the homegrown *Portland "400" Directory: A Residence Address, Visiting, Club, and Shopping Guide* of 1891 imitated East Coast social

Downtown in 1889. *Harper's Weekly* magazine in 1889 gave its readers a view of Front Avenue at its peak as the center of Portland's bustling commercial life. "One seeing Portland for the first time will be surprised to find how well-built it is," commented the magazine—a note that Eastern journalists would sound repeatedly over the next century and a quarter. (Author's collection)

registers and helped the "right people" identify each other. Elegant private parties, chronicled in the diary of Judge Matthew Deady, replaced the less sophisticated socializing of the 1860s and 1870s.

Families with leisure could follow the new fad of vigorous outdoor recreation by joining the new Multnomah Amateur Athletic Club (1891) and Waverly Golf Club (1896). There were picnics on Ross Island, day trips on Portland's rivers, and weeklong or even summer-long retreats at the new resorts of Seaside and Gearhart, Oregon, and Seaview, Washington, located at the ocean ends of rail lines. The hardiest Portlanders trekked to Cloud Cap Inn on Mount Hood or joined the Mazamas, whose inaugural climb on July 19, 1894, took 158 men and 38 women to the top of Mount Hood.

Not everyone could take a weekend to climb Mount Hood, but anyone could join the bicycle craze. More than a thousand cyclists paraded through downtown Portland on July 4, 1895, earning prizes for the most striking decorations. On Sundays thousands of people took to the roads and boulevards on cycling expeditions—sedate families, daredevil wheelmen, and "scorchers," young men who rode too fast and too recklessly for most people's taste. The *Cyclist's Road Map of Portland District* (1896) could be had for 50 cents. The more extensive *Road Book of Oregon*, published by the League of American Wheelmen in 1897, was free to members of the Oregon Division of the Wheelmen but cost a hefty $2 for others. There was even a short-lived Cycle Park on vacant land on the north rim of Sullivan's Gulch, south of Halsey from Eighteenth to Twenty-Fourth. Promoter W. F. Nelson leased the land in 1897,

CARRIAGE ROAD UNDER INCLINE.

EIGHTEENTH STREET CABLE INCLINE TO PORTLAND HEIGHTS.

Cable car ramp. From 1890 to 1904, the Portland Cable Railway company operated a cable car line that ran south on Fifth from Union Station, west on Jefferson, and south on what is now Southwest Eighteenth to climb a 1,040-foot-long trestle to Portland Heights. The trestle opened the highlands to real estate development and was the best way to reach the new view lots until the predecessor of the Vista Bridge opened in 1904—the current Vista Bridge dates from 1925. (Portland City Archives, A 2004-002.6714; Gholston Collection) carved out cycle paths, and built a fenced amphitheater with a bandstand. He hoped to make money by putting on shows, like the spectacular on July 3, 1897, that featured trick bike riding, a ladies' military band, fancy roller skating, and Scottish highland dancing. Nelson was pretty much broke by the next year, but cyclists and neighbors continued to use the neglected park until the Glisan family developed it as Wasco Addition, where the first house went up in 1902.

Portlanders with money were careful to pick the right neighborhoods for their increasingly palatial houses. Many chose the South Park Blocks and streets to the west. Prominent Jewish families like Selling, Gevurtz, Frank, and Meier liked the proximity to downtown stores and to Temple Beth Israel at Twelfth and Main. Novelist Nancy Noon Kendall, who grew up at Twelfth and Market, imagined a group of New England families who built on "the Park" in the 1880s because "everyone of importance" lived nearby. Their new houses had "enormous high-ceilinged rooms and vast halls carved down their middles" with "front parlors, back parlors, libraries, and dining rooms," perhaps decorated with marbles and bronzes brought back from tours of Europe.

The Park Blocks had competition. By the 1890s, Portland's business and civic leaders were moving to the western edge of town—especially to King's Hill, directly west of the city center, and to Nob Hill or "Nineteenth Street" in the northwest district. In the latter districts, double-size blocks gave the space necessary for "substantial comfort and display" in the words of Harvey Scott, who continued his description:

> One is led rapidly on by the sight of grand and imposing residences in the distance, of costly structure and splendid ornamentation. Many of these are set upon whole blocks, beautifully supplied with trees, turf, and flowers, and supplied with tasteful driveways . . . costing about $20,000 to $50,000—some of them $90,000 each—of three and four stories, and mainly in the Queen Anne style. It is upon the swell of the plateau that these fine houses begin to appear, and the views from their upper windows and turrets are extensive . . . the region is, by popular consent—and still more by prevailing prices—forever dedicated to dwellings of wealth and beauty.

Between Nob Hill and the Park Blocks, however, was the very different Goose Hollow neighborhood. Portland was still a tightly packed city in which walking was the most common means of transportation and the social character of neighborhoods changed block by block. Occupying lower land along Tanner Creek, Goose Hollow was like similar "flats" or "bottoms" neighborhoods in other cities, with ill-drained land occupied by poor people and shanty housing. The radical journalist John Reed dreaded walking through the area as a child in the 1890s: "My way to school ran through a sort of slum district, called Goose Hollow, peopled with brutal Irish boys . . . I was literally frightened out of my sense when I went through Goose Hollow." Other residents were Chinese gardeners who cultivated lands along the creek between Washington and Jefferson (until they were gradually pushed aside by the Multnomah Athletic Club and other development in the new century). Some sold their produce door to door from baskets dangling from the ends of long poles across their shoulders.

Downtown Portland also made a mixed impression on visitors. *Harper's Weekly* struck a positive note in 1889, writing that "one seeing Portland for the first time will be surprised to find how well-built it is." Rudyard Kipling, stopping in the city on a long journey from India to England in the same year, had a different take, finding a city of 50,000 people but very few pavements. "Portland is so busy," he commented, "that it can't attend to its own sewage or paving, and the four-storey brick blocks front cobble-stones and plank sidewalks and other things much worse." It was a great place to make money, he thought, but excessive willingness to put a dollar value on everything kept the town several measures short of "civilization." His impression of Portland didn't improve until he took a sightseeing voyage though the Columbia Gorge and fished the Clackamas River.

The 1890s did see the completion of three landmark buildings that might have pleased Kipling. After a false start in the 1880s, the Portland Hotel opened in 1890 on the block now occupied by Pioneer Courthouse Square. With eight floors and 326 sleeping rooms, it was immediately recognized as one of the finest hotels on the West Coast. Workers had City Hall ready for business on January 2, 1895. The new building was more attractive and less costly than the five-towered monster that the city had started to build in 1890. A first effort to build a proper railroad station had stalled in 1883, but Union Station (originally Grand Central Station) opened for travelers on February 14, 1896. The site had once been the wetland known as Couch Lake, where fifty years earlier Captain John Couch had been able to bag ducks for the dinner table from his front porch.

The building boom in the years around 1890 also gave Portland's in-fluential families some churches worthy of a major city. The wooden spire of Calvary Presbyterian—now preserved and restored as the Old Church—was adequate for 1882, but leaders of the burgeoning city soon preferred to

Portland Hotel construction. The Portland Hotel, completed after various fits and starts in 1890, gave the city its first luxury accommodations to match those of Eastern cities, although it would be well out of date by the time it was demolished in 1951. It was one of the most impressive construction projects in the city's early decades. Along with the railroads, the hotel was one of the major sources of employment for African Americans at the turn of the last century. (Gholston Collection)

worship in grander buildings. The First Congregational, First Presbyterian, First Baptist, and St. James Lutheran, as well as Temple Beth Israel congregations, all occupied new stone or brick buildings in a district located west of the business center, from the Park Blocks to Thirteenth Street.

The city's cultural institutions were as much the responsibility and prerogative of its upper class as were its economic decisions. The Library Association of Portland operated the city's main library on a subscription basis; 625 members paid $5 a year in 1895, reduced from $9 because of the depression. Contributions of $10,000 each from Henry Failing and Simeon Reed, added to generous bequests, allowed the library to move its 20,000 volumes into a new building at Stark and Broadway in 1893. Eastern library expert R. R. Bowker called it the finest such building on the coast. The new Art Association opened a small gallery of reproductions in 1895, using Ladd and Corbett dollars for its own building in 1905.

The same list of established families provided much of the support for private charity, responding to the growing problems of the city, although still lagging behind needs in the hard years of the mid-1890s. More often than not, they followed the leadership of Thomas Lamb Eliot, pastor of the First Unitarian Church. He pushed the organization of the Boys and Girls Aid Society in 1885 and the citywide Board of Charities, which coordinated volunteer efforts, in 1889. Like the Children's Home, which dated from the 1870s, these projects were commendable but limited attempts to treat specific symptoms rather than the larger problem of economic inequality. More valuable in the long run were experimental night schools for working men and boys sponsored by the YMCA, and similar schools for working girls sponsored by the Portland Women's League. The school board adopted the classes in 1889 at the urging of superintendent Ella Sabin.

It was the people on top who formulated Portland's late-19th-century image of livability with advantages "as a place to reside, as a place to engage in business, and as a place enjoying the requisite educational and social attributes necessary for the proper rearing of a family," in the words of a pamphlet entitled *Portland Oregon in 1900*. Portland meant good health, pure water, clean streets, pleasant homes, and, by the early 20th century, roses in abundance. It also meant thousands of immigrants, itinerant workers, and a bustling harbor with ships taking on lumber and wheat—the favorite illustration for articles about the city. In the first decades of the 20th century Portland would fulfill its promise as what Henry W. Corbett called "a modern city of great wealth, and of truly metropolitan importance."

Chapter 4
The Fair and the City

Portlanders loved a parade. Before movies and television, parades were a major form of entertainment, grand spectacles that brought citizens together to share the excitement of city life. In 1890, Harvey Scott noted that "scarcely a day passes but thick or thin files of men, accompanied by drum and brass band and banners, march to and fro." There were torch-light processions for political candidates. There were parades that included hundreds of cyclists during the bicycle craze of the 1890s, and parades featuring dozens of proud automobilists in the next decade. In June 1907, Portland staged the first annual Rose Festival with three days of pageantry. The procession included twenty illuminated floats built on flatcars carried on the trolley system.

One of the grandest parades of that era started at the corner of Sixth and Montgomery at 10 a.m. on June 1, 1905. Mounted police and a detachment of U.S. Cavalry led off, followed by marching bands, 2,000 National Guardsmen, and more police to bring up the rear. As the marchers trooped up Sixth, their ranks opened in front of the elegant Portland Hotel to make way for the carriages of visiting congressmen, governors, and Vice President Charles Fairbanks. Their destination was northwest Portland and the inaugural ceremony for the Lewis and Clark Centennial Exposition, where the opening-day crowd of 40,000 could listen to nearly a dozen long speeches about the importance of Portland and its world's fair.

Visitors who drifted away from the oratory discovered 400 acres of fairgrounds planned around the shallow waters of Guild's Lake. The formal layout imitated the "White City" of Chicago's magnificent Columbian Exposition in 1893. The majority of the exposition's buildings overlooked the lake from the bluff on which the Montgomery Ward warehouse later stood. A wide staircase led down the slope to the lake and "The Trail," the amusement arcade where the wonders of the world were available for a dime or a quarter. A "Bridge of Nations" connected the mainland to the United States government buildings, which were situated on a peninsula in the middle of the lake. For no apparent reason, the major exhibition halls followed the Spanish Renaissance style, with domes, cupolas, arched doorways, and red roofs. The federal building was built in a style that combined the architectural features of a railroad depot and a Mexican cathedral. The whitewashed stucco of the light frame buildings gleamed against the West Hills in the occasional Portland sun—like "diamonds set in a coronet of emeralds," according to one speaker.

From June 1 through October 15, nearly 1.6 million people paid for admission to the fair. Four hundred thousand of them were from beyond the Pacific Northwest. They could attend high-minded conferences on education, civic affairs, and the future of the United States in the Orient or participate in national conventions of librarians, social workers, physicians, and railroad conductors. They could inspect the exhibits of 16 states and 21 foreign nations. They could fritter their money on such carnival-like exhibits as "The Streets of Cairo" and "Professor Barnes' Educated Horse and Diving Elk" (the latter plunged into a tank of water from a 40-foot ramp). They could listen to band concerts or gape at the Forestry Building, the "world's largest log cabin." Constructed entirely of undressed logs, the "cabin" stretched 105 feet by 209 feet. The visitor entered through a portico of natural tree trunks into a vast interior modeled on the nave of a cathedral, with colonnades of tree trunks supporting the high ceiling and setting off balconies and exhibition galleries filled with samples of lumber, dioramas of elk and panthers, and photographs of American Indians by Edward Curtis. The largest foundation logs weighed in at 32 tons and measured 54 feet long and 5 feet across.

The city's business leadership gave wholehearted support to the planning and promotion of the Lewis and Clark Exposition because its purpose was a bigger and better Portland. It happened during an age when every ambitious city aspired to put on a national or international exposition. The list from recent decades already included Chicago, Omaha, Buffalo, St. Louis, Atlanta, and Nashville; it would soon add Norfolk, Seattle, San Francisco, and San Diego. At the least, a well-planned and successful event would show Easterners that Portland was a mature and "finished" city rather than a frontier town. At most it could give Portland an edge in the ongoing competition with upstart Seattle and confirm the city as a commercial center for the Pacific Northwest.

When Oregonians in the 21st century speak about the importance of trade with the Pacific Rim, they are reiterating ideas that were common eighty years ago. The official title of the event was the Lewis and Clark

Lewis and Clark Exposition. The Lewis and Clark Exposition turned marshes and dairy land on the edge of the city into a temporary wonderland of gardens, lath-and-plaster exhibition buildings tarted up to look like marble, and an amusement midway that was a sort of living *National Geographic* magazine. Because the Exposition company leased rather than purchased the land, Portland did not benefit from the legacy of a new park, as Chicago, St. Louis, and San Diego did after their world's fairs—or even a university campus, as was the case in Seattle. (Oregon Historical Society, Neg 36787)

Centennial Exposition and Oriental Fair. The motto over the entrance gate was "Westward the Course of Empire Takes Its Way." The biggest foreign exhibit came from Japan. As Exposition president Henry Goode explained, the first large international fair on the West Coast would "demonstrate to the commercial world . . . the actual inception of the era of new trade relations with the teeming millions of Asiatic countries." Even Portland's prestigious *Pacific Monthly* took time out from publishing stories by Jack London and essays by John Muir to tell readers about Portland's role in "The Coming Supremacy of the Pacific." A visiting journalist agreed that "the whole fair is a successful effort to express . . . the natural richness of the country and its relative nearness to Asia."

American supremacy on the Pacific included domination of the Philippines, which were acquired from Spain and pacified with a nasty colonial war between 1899 and 1902. The upshot for the Exposition was an embarrassing episode in which backwoods Filipinos were imported to serve as a live anthropology exhibit. Twenty-five Igorrote villagers arrived in early September to take up residence in a hastily constructed "village." What fairgoers learned about these people of the new Pacific America was that they were pagans and barbarians who knew to "obey the white man implicitly" and that they did not normally wear many clothes, but had to put up with American modesty while they were in Portland. And their diet in the Philippines sometimes included dogs, a fact that gave Oregonians endless amusement. "We saw the dog-eaters," one Portlander recorded in her diary, "and had just lots of

Sacagawea statue. Advocates for women's rights helped to raise the funds for a statue commemorating Sacagawea as part of the Lewis and Clark Exposition. It was unveiled at the Fair in 1905, with suffrage advocate Susan B. Anthony in attendance, and was subsequently moved to Washington Park, where Sacagawea points forever westward to the Pacific. (Photo by author)

fun." Unmentioned was the fact that Meriwether Lewis, William Clark, and their companions had also eaten dogs on their long trek a century earlier.

American Indians were also present at the fair, and also in a subordinate position. The most prominent presence of Native Americans was inanimate — the bronze statue of Sacagawea that would later stand in Washington Park. The Indian exhibit in the Government Building publicized the training programs at government-run schools like Chemawa in Salem. "This is the first exhibition of Indian work made on the Pacific Coast where the general public have had the opportunity of examining the character of the training given people in the Government Indian schools," said the official program. A Pacific Coast Institute brought together staff from the various Indian schools to discuss practical issues of administration and curriculum. Portland housewives might have been happy to learn from the Institute that Indian girls could be trained as "neat and capable housekeepers" for upper-class families.

Civic boosters had plenty to crow about. The Exposition, in the words of *Harper's Weekly*, "marked the close of an old epoch and the beginning of a new one for Portland." The Exposition had helped launch a boom in both business and population. Skyrocketing prices in downtown real estate made speculators rich and millionaires richer. The annual value of new construction quintupled between 1905 and 1910. Portland's population passed 200,000 by 1910 and may have reached 225,000 by 1913, when the boom finally ended.

Much of the new investment was centered downtown, which was literally growing up with the city. Architects in New York, Chicago, and Minneapolis had begun to experiment with iron and steel frames for tall buildings in the early 1880s. Elevators steadily became faster and safer in the 1890s, with electric power and after 1902 with gearless traction systems that allowed faster service to higher floors. Investors loved elevators because they could now charge full rent, or even a premium, for top-floor offices.

Portland was no Chicago, but taller buildings began to rise above the walk-up downtown. Two serious floods had changed the dynamics of downtown real estate. Fifteen days of rain in February 1890 had given Front and First streets a "decidedly Venetian look." Four years later, May rains and rapid snowmelt pushed water as far west as Third and Washington, and on June 1 the *Oregonian* reported "a large flotilla of boats of all sizes on Stark Street," although businesses improvised wooden walkways and continued to operate out of upper floors. The upshot was to make Fourth, Fifth, and Sixth streets look like safer sites for investment than locations closer to the river. Real estate values reached $5,000 a front foot in the heart of the new window-shopping district along Alder and Washington. Soon ten-story office towers were springing up all over downtown—sixteen of them by 1920—many of them clad with white or tan terra-cotta tiles that reflected the winter sun and brightened the streets. Local architects were certainly pleased when Herbert Croly, editor of the *Architectural Record*, gave the city high marks for its architectural sophistication when he visited in 1912.

The Exposition had been a celebration of electricity as well as commerce, and Portlanders entered the new century ready to make the most of the new technology. Foreshadowing the great regional hydropower system that would be built in the 1930s, 1940s, and 1950s, Portland was an electrical pioneer. Within a year after Thomas Edison invented the incandescent light in 1879, railroad promoter Henry Villard had moored his ship *Columbia* at the foot of Flanders Street and decked it out with electric lights powered onboard the ship. Sawmill owner George Weidler had installed a dynamo at his northwest Portland factory for arc lighting and supplied power to businesses that wanted their own lights. On June 3, 1889, in an event of nationwide significance, direct current at commercial strength was transmitted for the first time over a long-distance line that stretched 14 miles from Willamette Falls at Oregon City to Portland (alternating current was first transmitted in September 1890). In 1885, Portland City Council thought it was being thoroughly modern by replacing coal-oil street lamps with five hundred gas lights at $1,600 per year. They were supposed to burn from twilight to midnight. Twenty years later, downtown streets were being lit with suspended festoons of electric bulbs.

Businesses were early adopters of electric light for display windows, signs, and work spaces. Residential lighting worked its way down the economic ladder and outward from the center of town. In a complaint that sounds familiar today, residents of St. Johns in 1904 objected that the power company was neglecting them for closer, more lucrative customers. After lighting the parlor, households could begin to consider electric appliances. By 1905 and 1906, Portland Railway, Light and Power, or PRL&P, was advertising electric irons (both the "Regular Household, 6-lb Flat Iron" and the "Nickel Plated, 3-pound, Smoothing Iron"), tea kettles, chafing dishes, fans, and other appliances. Other ads urged storekeepers to "burn your name into the public mind—use an electric sign" because electric lighting "will boom your business by causing your store to stand out more prominently than its neighbors." Because PRL&P president Henry Goode was also president of the Lewis and Clark Exposition, the buildings at the 1905 fair were bordered by electric lights that shimmered at night in the placid water of Guild's Lake. Up in the West Hills was a 30-by-100-foot electric sign proclaiming "1905" that could reportedly be read from 30 miles away.

Portland's headlong prosperity depended on its roles as trade center and port. In 1891, the state legislature had created the Port of Portland to maintain and improve harbor facilities. Given the city's situation as a river port, the agency's most important service was to maintain the channel in the Willamette. It also operated a dry dock and improved towing and pilotage services. Meanwhile, the Army Corps of Engineers had begun to improve the dangerous mouth of the Columbia in 1884. Between 1903 and 1917, the Corps deepened the bar channel to 37 feet and maintained a minimum depth of 26 feet upriver.

Local manufacturing expanded in the same years, especially in the realms of lumber, wood products, and furniture, but the biggest growth was in trade and transportation. James J. Hill, the railroad magnate who had built the Great Northern Railroad and made the fortunes of Puget Sound cities, started work on a North Bank railroad (the Spokane, Portland, and Seattle) from Pasco to

Harvey Scott statue. Harvey Scott, editor of the *Oregonian* from 1865 to 1910 (with one five-year break) was an inveterate booster of Portland and a rock-solid advocate of conservative political values. In this chunky bronze by Gutzom Borglum he looks appropriately judgmental and combatative, to use the adjectives of historian Lee Nash. The statue at the pinnacle of Mount Tabor Park ironically faces east, toward the old Atlantic world, rather than west toward the new world of the Pacific that he so often promoted. (Photo by author)

Portland in 1906. Completion of the road in 1908 gave the Northern Pacific and Great Northern railroads independent access to Portland.

Within a few years, Hill was locked into one of the last great railroad-building contests, in which the adversaries vied to tap the lumber and cattle country of central Oregon. "James J. Hill Spends Millions to Tap Interior" read one headline in the *Oregonian* describing the line he built up along the Deschutes River. "Harriman Road Has 2,600 Men at Work" trumpeted another article in the same issue. "Harriman" was E. H. Harriman, who controlled both the Union Pacific and Southern Pacific railways. After open warfare in the Deschutes Canyon, the two tycoons struck a deal and the rails reached Bend in 1911.

Now that the city had a link to the interior, Portland bankers financed the developing cattle, wool, and grain businesses of the Inland Empire. Wheat farmers had begun pushing south from the Columbia River in the 1880s and were now supporting new towns such as Wasco and Moro. Sheepherders traded their wool at Shaniko at the terminus of the Columbia and Southern Railroad. Hood River orchardists sawed down the Douglas fir trees that filled the valley, killing the stumps with arsenic and planting apple trees. Swift and

Wells Fargo Building and Sixth Avenue, 1910. In 1910, the Wells Fargo Building was one of Portland's newest and most impressive skyscrapers. Designed by Benjamin Wistar Morris III, a native Portlander practicing architecture in New York, it set a stylish tone with smooth tan brick and bright terra-cotta additions to the façade. The building helped to establish Sixth Avenue as the heart of Portland's booming downtown. (Portland City Archives—Gaston)

Company built a huge new meat-packing plant in North Portland. Headlines in a special issue of the *Oregonian* on January 1, 1910, told of the excitement: "Wheat Output Will Be Enormous"; "Interior Towns Face Bright Future"; "Oregon Forging to Front as Livestock State."

Steam-powered logging was simultaneously transforming the Coast Range and the slopes of the Cascades. New "steam donkey" engines to winch logs out of the woods didn't mire down in wet weather like ox teams. Timber companies built dozens of short logging railroads up small valleys to tap previously isolated stands. Maps from the first quarter of the century show temporary lines reaching up from the coast and the Columbia like the veins of a leaf. The changes were part of a great regional shift in the timber industry. With the best timberlands of the Northeast and the Great Lakes states logged over by the end of the 19th century, timber tycoons looked to the vast forests of the Northwest. The most famous event in this shift was the decision of Frederick Weyerhaeuser of Minnesota in 1900 to buy 900,000 acres of timberland from the Northern Pacific Railroad and relocate to the Northwest. By 1905, Washington ranked first in lumber production and Oregon soon took second place. The Northwest share of national lumber production jumped from 8 percent to 20 percent in the single decade of 1900 to 1910.

Portland wholesalers supplied the farmers, ranchers, and loggers with tools and tobacco. Portland longshoremen loaded the ships that made the city one of the nation's leading ports for the export of lumber and wheat. Insurance agents, railroad hands, draymen, carpenters, lawyers, retail clerks—nearly everyone benefited from the growth of Portland's commercial empire.

Voters took steps to assure that growth in 1910, when they approved a charter amendment creating a Commission of Public Docks. Portland's waterfront in the early 20th century was in the tight grip of the railroads, which had a limited interest in promoting maritime trade. Private owners controlled every functioning dock, whether in northwest Portland or on the east side. Most had been built for the coastwise trade to California and were inadequate for transoceanic shipping. Under the direction of Portland's business establishment, the Docks Commission opened Municipal Dock No. 1 on North Front Street in 1914. A major motivation for the annexation of the independent city of St. Johns in 1915 was to enable the Docks Commission to fund the improvement of the St. Johns city dock. Still to come in the 1920s was the Port of Portland's massive dredging project that shifted the Willamette channel from the east side of Swan Island to the west.

The boom years also opened regular employment to thousands of Portland women, who made up only 15 percent of the city's wage earners in

1900 but 24 percent by 1920. Women dominated half a dozen job categories, ranging from servant to dressmaker to boardinghouse keeper. By 1910 more than 2,000 women worked in the lower-paying professions as nurses, music teachers, musicians, and schoolteachers, and 6,000 more worked in white-collar jobs as "typewriters," stenographers, salespeople, telephone operators, and clerks.

In the early years of the century, thousands of other Portland women earned their livelihoods, in full or in part, from prostitution. In 1893, the Portland Ministerial Association found prostitution concentrated in the parlor houses and saloons of the North End and waterfront. Rich and poor alike, Portland's men could indulge in drink, gambling, and illicit sex as a single vice because, according to a report by the Ministerial Association, "saloons and houses of ill-fame were generally combined in the same building." In 1907 and 1908, new ordinances barring women from saloons and stringent law enforcement by a reform administration forced many prostitutes out of the houses and into the roles of streetwalker and call girl. Still, the Vice Commission in 1912 found more than four hundred downtown hotels, apartment buildings, and lodging houses that condoned or encouraged use by an estimated three thousand "sporting women" (although their definition clearly included women who enjoyed casual sex, in addition to professional prostitutes).

Middle-class and working-class families who wanted to keep themselves carefully separated from the seamy neighborhoods around the business district could thank the expansion of the electrified transit system that made it easy to reach outlying neighborhoods. Backroom deals and Wall Street buyouts brought more than a dozen separate companies into a single streetcar monopoly in 1906. The Portland Railway Light and Power Company (PRL&P) operated 161 miles of railway and six electric power plants and carried 16 million passengers by 1910. In that year a thousand streetcars a day rattled and clanked across the Willamette bridges. The trolleys entered downtown from the east on Morrison Street and from the west on Washington, creating a miniature version of Chicago's Loop and defining the best location for the Meier and Frank, Lipman-Wolfe, and Olds, Wortman, and King department stores. The volume of streetcar traffic quadrupled in the first decade of the century, and Portlanders hopped on trolleys twice as often as they had a few years earlier. So many streetcars and wagons crowded Third Street that the city stationed its first traffic-control officer at its intersection with Washington in 1901.

Dozens of electric interurban railroads that stimulated the growth of a suburban ring between 5 and 15 miles from the center of town complemented

Hotel Broadway. Built in 1913 at the corner of Burnside and Broadway, the structure was part of a hotel building frenzy in downtown Portland as the city grew and railroad travel boomed in the early 20th century. Blocks close to Union Station filled with respectable but economical hotels like the Broadway. Travelers with money could opt for upscale accommodations in the $2 million Multnomah Hotel (now Embassy Suites) or the elegant Oregon Hotel, soon renamed for its owner Simon Benson. (Portland City Archives, A 2001-062.12)

the Portland streetcar system. At the height of the interurban system in 1915, the suburban division of PRL&P ran to Troutdale, Gresham, Boring, Estacada, and Oregon City. Oregon Electric, controlled by James Hill's railroad empire, ran one line to Beaverton, Hillsboro, and Forest Grove and a second through Tualatin and Wilsonville to Salem and Eugene. The Southern Pacific Red Electrics ran to Garden Home, Beaverton, and Hillsboro before swinging south to McMinnville and Corvallis.

Streetcar and interurban companies generated their own traffic by building parks and amusement centers alongside the lines. In the early 1900s, before the typical family owned a Model-T, summer weekends and holidays meant packing a picnic basket and fishing gear for an interurban excursion to Canemah Park above Willamette Falls, Estacada Recreation Park on the Clackamas River, or Dodge Park on the line to the Bull Run power plant. Closer to town were Oaks Amusement Park, featuring concerts, vaudeville acts, a skating rink, rides, and food; and Council Crest Park, whose roller coaster gave the best views in the city to riders who were brave enough to open their eyes. As historian Sara Paulson notes, management portrayed Oaks Amusement Park as "The People's Park" for the respectable working

Madison Bridge workers. Well into the 20th century, building Portland was a pick-and-shovel project in which teams of workers used steam power, horse power, and their own muscles to build and maintain the growing network of bridges, streets, and utilities that held the city together. These workers posed on the Madison Bridge in 1910. (Portland City Archives, A 2004-002.1)

class and "a pleasure place where your children may romp with you every day in the week in peace and safety; where you will be personally anxious to bring your friends, and a place to which, as a loyal citizen, you may proudly point to and say, This is typical of Portland."

Prosperity plus new streetcar lines provided the impetus for a residential real-estate boom that surpassed even the subdivision mania of the late 1880s and early 1890s. The list of new developments between 1904 and 1910 includes dozens of names familiar to Portlanders. With relatively level land suitable for trolleys, the east side continued to monopolize residential growth in old neighborhoods and in new entries such as Overlook, Montavilla, Rose City Park, Gregory Heights, Kenton, Beaumont, and Westmoreland. The most exclusive new developments were Alameda Park (1909), Laurelhurst (1909), and Eastmoreland (1910). The 1920s would see the rapid development of Council Crest, Burlingame, Arlington Heights, Willamette Heights, and other new plats in the West Hills.

The Exposition boom helped to make Portland into a city of home-owners. In 1900, Portland had 14,625 dwelling units for a census count of 16,334 families. By 1910, it had 37,426 dwelling units—meaning that builders had erected 21,000 new houses and apartments! Furthermore, 28 percent of families owned their homes free and clear and another 18 percent were paying off mortgages. Portland ended the first decade of the new century fifth among large cities in the percentage of households that owned or were buying their own houses. Only Akron, Grand Rapids, Spokane, and Oakland ranked higher.

The boom also built an "eastside" city. For a decade, virtually all the new housing was built on the east side, and the population balance between the two parts of the city tipped toward the east as early as 1906. In 1916 the telephone company estimated that there were two eastsiders for every westsider. In addition to St. Johns, other eastside neighborhoods—including Mount Tabor, Montavilla, Rose City Park, Woodstock, Eastmoreland, and Mount Scott—chose annexation to the city to assure good water and streetcar service.

Private developers made money by selling lots and by providing streetcar service to and from the new residents' homes. It was these new property owners, however, who footed the bill for the expanded public services needed because of rapid development. A second water pipeline from Bull Run to a second storage reservoir at Mount Tabor cost taxpayers $1,720,000 in 1911. The bill for streets and sewers came to $28 million from 1905 through 1914, compared to $8 million for the previous *four* decades. The development of

Sandy Boulevard. The streetcar city is under construction along Northeast Sandy Boulevard at Fifty-Seventh in the 1910s. Speculative commercial buildings are going up adjacent to the streetcar line, while small builders fill in the nearby residential blocks a few houses at a time. (Oregon Historical Society Neg 81110).

Laurelhurst. The 1910s brought a set of new neighborhoods designed for upscale families in business and the professions. Laurelhurst, Alameda, and Eastmoreland shared gently curving streets, boulevards, and well-marked boundaries that set them apart from middling neighborhoods. The letterhead for the Laurelhurst Company showed street trees far larger than the actual saplings of the 1910s and assured potential buyers about their "high-class" neighbors. Left unsaid was the fact that restrictive covenants written into the deeds prohibited sales to Asian Americans and African Americans; the U.S. Supreme Court would declare such restrictions legally unenforceable in 1948. (Gholston Collection)

new neighborhoods also brought the need to link residents with downtown jobs. The replacement of three old bridges and the construction of the new Broadway Bridge in 1913 cost $4.5 million.

During the same years, a remarkable set of sharp, energetic women were shaping key cultural institutions, taking advantage of the expanding opportunities for women to attend college, gain professional training, and build national careers. Mary Frances Isom directed what became the Multnomah County Library from 1901 to 1920, overseeing its transition from a private organization to a free library (utilizing legislation pushed by the Oregon Federation of Women's Clubs). She worked with architect A. E. Doyle to make sure that the new Central Library building was one of the most modern and innovative in the country when it opened in 1913. Anna Belle Crocker similarly shepherded the transition of the elite Portland Art Association into the Portland Art Museum as its curator from 1909 to 1936. She also supervised a key construction project—the new museum that Pietro Belluschi designed for the South Park Blocks, which opened in 1932. Crocker also ran the Museum Art School, while well-connected Julia Hoffman was founding and driving the development of the Oregon School of Arts and Crafts from 1907 to 1936.

The Board of Park Commissioners dated to 1900, when the city decided it needed systematic management of Washington Park, Macleay Park, and smaller properties. Under the leadership of Thomas Lamb Eliot, the Unitarian minister and social reformer who was as much an environmentalist as he was a crusader, the board split the cost of hiring landscape architect John Olmsted with the Exposition Company. For a total of $10,000, Portland bought the design for the Exposition grounds and its first comprehensive park plan from the nation's premier firm of landscape planners. John Olmsted followed in the footsteps of his stepfather, Frederick Law Olmsted, who had designed New York's Central Park, and he continued the family landscape architecture and planning business. His ideas for Portland included small playgrounds and neighborhood parks as well as the improvement of large rural and suburban tracts and the development of parkways. He wanted the city to turn the wetlands along the Columbia and at Ross Island, Guild's Lake, and Swan Island into expansive park reserves. A loop of smaller parks and parkways would line the West Hills and connect the bluffs and ridges of the east side.

T. L. Eliot is worth an extra look—he is, after all, the only person to lend his name to both a Mount Hood glacier and a Reed College building. Eliot arrived in Portland in 1867 at age 26 as pastor for a growing Unitarian congregation, which he served until health forced him to retire in 1893. Both before and after retirement, he took the lead in making Portland a humane city. He served several years as superintendent for Multnomah County public schools, founded the Children's Home for orphans and the Boys and Girls Aid Society, supported votes for women and basic rights for prisoners, and served on the boards of the Library Association and Reed College. His work on the Parks Commission was part of a larger interest in the outdoors that took him to Mount Hood many times and led to his name being bestowed upon the mountain's most massive glacier.

Portlanders thought that Olmsted's ideas were fine, but feared that the price would be steeper than the hillside parks. A $1 million bond issue paid for three miles of Terwilliger Boulevard and secured public ownership of Laurelhurst, Sellwood, Mount Tabor, and Peninsula parks before the money ran out in 1910. But voters turned their thumbs down on new park spending in the 1910s. Most of the riverfront land that Olmsted had allocated for parks went to industry and airports over the following decades. Parkways seemed of less importance than roads as the automobile took over as the primary mode of transportation. The vast expanse of Forest Park is the result of public foreclosure of tax delinquent property during the Depression of the 1930s, not of systematic planning by the preceding generation.

As work lagged on the parks system, a meeting of planning enthusiasts in the fall of 1909 led to the formation of a group called the Civic Improvement League, which quickly raised $20,000 from private donors to hire an outside expert to formulate a comprehensive plan for making Portland an "ideal city." The League's major contributors and executive committee comprised a "who's who" of successful Portlanders. The planner who got the job

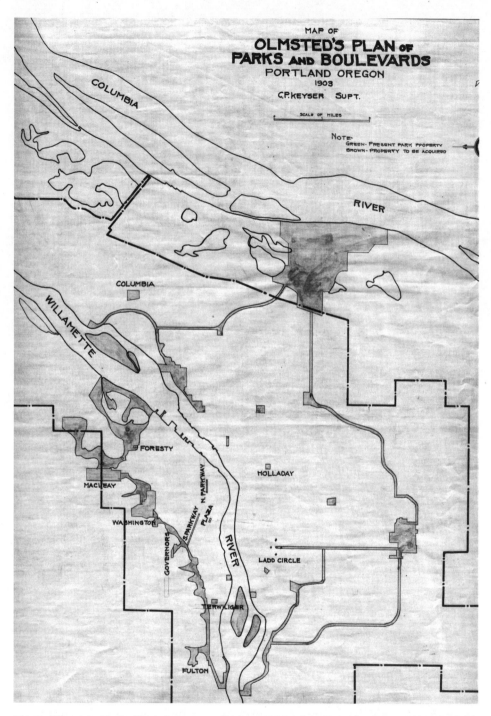

Olmsted Plan. John Charles Olmsted, stepson and business partner of the famous landscape architect Frederick Law Olmsted, prepared a comprehensive open space and boulevard plan for the Portland Parks Commission in 1903. He spent several days in carriage rides around the city with Commissioner Lester Hawkins and formed his impressions of a cityscape of extremes—steep, sometimes barren hills and extensive riverfront lands that were hard for real estate development but excellent for open space. The resulting plan has been a touchstone for parks advocates for more than a century since his visit. (Portland Parks Bureau)

Bennett Plan. Edward Bennett's 1911 plan for Greater Portland was both practical and grandiose. Along with practical proposals for wider streets, parks, and expanded marine terminals, it envisioned a Portland that imitated great European capitals like Budapest, Berlin, and Paris, with wide boulevards lined with tastefully imposing buildings. (Author's collection)

was Edward Bennett, a British-born architect who had assisted the famous Daniel Burnham in the preparation of landmark plans for Chicago and San Francisco. He received $500 a month and expenses in return for his expertise. Bennett presented his preliminary sketches to the Civic Improvement League in February 1911 and had the final plan ready by the end of the summer.

The plan worked outward from the center of the city. Anticipating an eventual metropolitan population of two million, Bennett called for three civic centers—government offices around City Hall for "nobility of appearance"; a transportation center including a post office and new railway station; and a cultural center with museum and auditorium below Washington Park. The plan suggested radial highways, parks, and parkways for the east side. New rail yards and docks would be built downstream, with the upper Willamette reclaimed for parks and pleasure boats in the style of Paris and Budapest.

Business and civic associations were enthusiastic. Mayor Allen G. Rushlight proclaimed February 29, 1912, as Greater Portland Day. Canvassers fanned out through the town at precisely 10:30 a.m. to kick off a membership drive that eventually sold 10,000 Greater Portland Plan buttons at one dollar each. The effort concluded with an evening parade on October 30 led by horn-tooting automobiles. The final step was to secure formal recognition by the voters, without asking them to allocate the necessary millions immediately. The vote on November 2, 1912, was 2 to 1 to approve Bennett's vision as Portland's official plan, to be followed as closely as possible so long as it was reasonable and practical.

Within weeks, Bennett's plan took a backseat in local politics to the campaign for a commission form of city government. The narrow vote that amended the city charter climaxed a decade of political turmoil, for the clean-scrubbed face that Portland put on for tourists and business at the Lewis and Clark Exposition masked backroom politics that were as corrupt as ever. Historian Gordon Dodds, in his *Oregon: A Bicentennial History*, described the alliance of "business interests, gamblers, and thugs" that ruled Portland in the interests of licit and illicit commerce behind the figurehead of George H. Williams, whose mayoral term lasted from 1902 to 1905. In an era of political bossism, Portland's version of the party boss was W. F. "Jack" Matthews, who pulled the strings in the city and state Republican parties while holding a series of patronage jobs and generally trying to keep his picture out of the papers. As muckraking journalist Burton Hendrick would write in *McClure's Magazine* in 1911, "the kind of government with which the Republican machine was identified was concretely illustrated in the municipal administration of Portland. Even on the Pacific Coast, Portland enjoyed a peculiar fame as a wide-open town . . . the city had become a popular headquarters for all the vicious characters in the Pacific Northwest."

Then, in 1904 and 1905, headline-making indictments and trials of leading politicians for involvement in schemes to obtain fraudulent title to timberlands shattered the Oregon machine. President Theodore Roosevelt removed Jack Matthews from his position as U.S. Marshal, thus creating a vacuum in local politics. The mayor's office was up for grabs. The reformer

Waterfront disrepair. In 1928-29, the city acted on one of the goals of the Bennett plan by demolishing rotting wharves and warehouses to build a flood control seawall and interceptor sewer in front of downtown. This picture looks south to the second Morrison Bridge, with the Hawthorne Bridge in the background. The interceptor sewer was a training-wheels version of the massive "Big Pipe" project of the early 21st century, while the seawall and land clearance behind it made space for Harbor Drive and then Waterfront Park. (Portland City Archives, A 1999-04.82)

who defeated Williams in 1905 was Dr. Harry Lane. A Democrat, Lane ran with the support of progressive businessmen, the *Oregon Journal*, and the respectable middle class. Grandson of Joseph Lane, Oregon's first territorial governor, Doc Lane was an outdoorsman of the Teddy Roosevelt mold who enjoyed making surprise visits to construction sites to find out for himself if the city was getting full value for its dollar. He was honest beyond question. When he later served in the U.S. Senate, colleagues called him "the human question mark" for his tendency to question federal spending. Lane vetoed scores of ordinances during his four years in office, but a city council that listened closely to liquor dealers and railroad executives usually overrode the vetoes on 13–2 votes. He lost most of his battles to preserve the public interest against the "big boys"—Portland Railway Light and Power; Jim Hill's Spokane, Portland, and Seattle Railroad; the Union Pacific; and the Southern Pacific. Lane's strongest support in 1905 and in his 1907 re-election campaign came from the skilled workers and middle-class homeowners of the east side, who worried about the political alliance between the moguls of the Heights and the economically marginal residents of the North End.

Indeed, historian Robert Johnston has argued persuasively that Lane was a voice of middle-class populism—even radicalism—that flourished among small-business proprietors, homeowners, and skilled workers, most of whom were residents of the young and fast-developing neighborhoods east of the Willamette River. Like the pieces in a kaleidoscope, different leaders, interest groups, and voters came together in a disparate set of political efforts that were linked by their defense of the right of ordinary citizens to determine their own future. The argument, in simplest terms, is that Portland's image as a conservative and staid city that avoided the social and political extremes of places like Seattle and San Francisco is inaccurate, less a reflection of actual experience than a myth that has served the interests of big business and property owners.

Organized labor was part of this middle-class populism. In 1908, several unions came together to form the Central Labor Council. The Portland *Labor Press* editorialized against business-oriented candidates. The Longshoremen's Union organized a Workingmen's Political Club to endorse sympathetic candidates. To the left of the craft unions was the Industrial Workers of the World (IWW), which advocated radical action and hoped to organize all workers into One Big Union. In 1907, the IWW led 3,000 sawmill workers in striking the Inman-Poulsen mill on the Southeast waterfront and the Eastern-Western Lumber Mill in Northwest. In 1913, women workers challenged the management of the Oregon Packing Company with IWW support. It is likely that IWW members also helped to elect a Socialist to represent St. Johns on the city council in 1912.

When Tammany Hall ward boss George Washington Plunkitt told a New York reporter that "reformers are only mornin' glories," he was talking about the resiliency of political machines and the general inability of middle-class reformers to parlay single electoral victories into permanent changes. He might well have been talking about Portland in 1909 and 1910 under the leadership of Mayor Joseph Simon. After Lane decided not to run for a third two-year term, Simon easily defeated reform-minded opponents despite active neighborhood groups and politically savvy unions. Coming to City Hall at the end of a 35-year career that had taken him as far as the U.S. Senate, Simon was the smoothest of Portland's professional politicians. In public he supported such respectable causes as park acquisition and the Bennett plan, while behind the scenes he guided a well-oiled political machine that made sure that big businesses were happy. Lane had pushed what we can call the east-side agenda by declaring war on prostitution in 1908, challenging the system of tacit licensing in which gambling houses and brothels paid monthly

Traffic control signal. Mayor Albee (left) stands proudly in 1915 beside the city's first traffic control signal at Southwest Third and Morrison—an early sign that the regulation of automobile traffic would prove one of the biggest headaches for municipal officials for the next century. (Portland City Archives, A 2005.005)

fines and continued to operate. Simon brought back the wide-open city and allowed vice to spread beyond the well-established red-light district.

The impetus for permanent change finally came from two objective reports. In the first, the 1912 Vice Commission appointed by new mayor Allen G. Rushlight compiled detailed documentation on the extent of prostitution, the ubiquity of venereal disease, and the complacent attitude of the police and courts. The report certainly did not surprise anyone who had ever walked around downtown Portland with open eyes, but the Vice Commission's building-by-building inventory and its candid interviews with scores of prostitutes were difficult to ignore. So was the conclusion that law enforcement amounted to informal licensing, when fines for prostitution and for maintaining a bawdy house averaged less than a good day's take.

For many businessmen and bankers, vice may have been embarrassing but government inefficiency was intolerable—not merely an insult to public morals, but an injury to every taxpayer. The second report that jolted Portland's establishment into action came in April 1913, when the New York Bureau of Municipal Research reported on an investigation of Portland's city government. Editor C. S. Jackson used his *Oregon Journal* to publicize its findings by detailing the operational problems of ten city departments. Only the water bureau got good marks. According to the report, the police department was disorganized, city accounting and budgeting departments were in shambles, health inspections were a sham and public works a scandal.

The impact of these reports prompted a call for the adoption of the commission form of government, as had been recently developed in Galveston, Texas. The proposed charter provided for nonpartisan elections, the abolishment of the ward system in favor of citywide elections, and the replacement of the mayor and city council with a mayor and four commissioners. Meeting together, the five would serve as the city's legislative body. Acting separately, each one would administer a city department and carry out the ordinances adopted as a group. The goal was to bring Portland a more businesslike and less expensive government by eliminating political horse-trading and ensuring coordination among departments. Liberal Republicans, planning enthusiasts, Roosevelt Progressives, and social reformers backed the change. Old guard Republicans, who were satisfied with their control of the local political machine, dug in their heels to resist the new charter. At the other end of the political spectrum, the *Labor Press* thought that workingmen should wait for more significant changes. In May 1913, Portland approved the charter—which has served since with minor changes—by 722 votes. The charter represented middle-class and working-class reform, with the margin of victory for progressive reform again coming from the east side.

Commission government meant government for homeowners, small businessmen, professionals, skilled workers, and the other members of Portland's great middle class. It also helped to set the city's tone for the next two generations. In the first years of the 20th century, Portland had been a rambunctious town caught up in the excitement of headlong growth. There were new opportunities to try, money to be made, and new communities to build. By the 1920s and 1930s, the city would slow down and grow more conservative, concerned with maintaining its obvious attractions rather than risking change. The city would continue to evolve, but more slowly and more cautiously, with an eye toward stable neighborhoods and low taxes.

Dissenters

In December 1915, radical journalist John Reed returned to his hometown of Portland for a brief family visit and swept Louise Bryant off her feet. There are multiple versions of the story of their first meeting (the version in the movie *Reds*, starring Warren Beatty and Diane Keaton, is just one of many). What we know for sure is that Reed had long since decided that Greenwich Village was far more exciting than Portland, which was "awful beyond words," and that Bryant was happy to second his opinion. She was on the train to New York three days after he left, abandoning her left-leaning husband and scandalizing even Portland's small circle of free-thinking intellectuals. For the next five years, until Reed's death, Reed and Bryant reported on the Russian Revolution and were considered Portland's most famous radicals, even though Reed would never return to the city and Bryant returned only once, in 1919, to urge an audience at the new Civic Auditorium to protest U.S. efforts to crush the Bolshevik revolution.

John Reed and Louise Bryant were networkers before the term was coined, and their time in Portland opens windows onto the passionate and often disorganized world of Portland dissenters in the early 20th century.

For many in the Industrial Workers of the World (whose members were known as Wobblies), Portland was a stopover and temporary home as they followed jobs and organizing drives from city to city and state to state. William Z. Foster, later a key leader of the Communist Party USA, worked out of Portland from 1901 to 1907 on the docks and in lumber camps, and joined the IWW in 1909. A year later, Joe Hillstrom wrote a letter to the IWW newspaper in which he identified himself as a member of the Portland local, condemned the brutality of Portland police, and signed himself "Joe Hill." He would soon bring his famous song "The Preacher and the Slave," with its promise of "pie in the sky when you die," to a local IWW meeting. Hill was likely the sort of person Reed had in mind when he commented that "in my native place . . . the IWW Hall was the liveliest intellectual center in town."

If Wobblies like Joe Hill wanted to tear down the system and start over, the women who campaigned for the right to vote wanted to change it from within. The driving wheel of the suffrage campaign was the indefatigable Abigail Scott Duniway—novelist, magazine editor, tireless campaigner, and perpetual opponent of her brother Harvey Scott, who edited the *Oregonian* as the voice of the status quo. Her signature line was "Yours for Liberty" and her journal *The New Northwest* proclaimed its goal to be "Free Speech, Free Press, Free People." By the teens of the new century, Duniway was a

respected veteran of the women's rights campaign, which she had been spark-
ing since 1871, but younger women like Louise Bryant and Sara Bard Field
joined in lecture tours that helped to make Oregon the seventh state to adopt
women's suffrage in 1912.

Sara Bard Field offers one connection to Charles Erskine Scott Wood
and John Reed another. To Reed, Wood was an informal mentor and influence; to Field, he was a lover and eventual life companion. Wood himself was a
man of expansive energy and interests. He was an army officer who fought the
Nez Perce and befriended Chief Joseph, a lawyer who made a small fortune
working for local business leaders and foreign investors, a painter, and a poet.
He was also, as the 1900s turned into the 1910s, an increasingly vocal dissenter
in local politics, working against racial and gender discrimination, supporting
the Wobblies, and defending the free-speech rights of anarchist Emma Gold-
man and birth-control activist Margaret Sanger. In 1918, increasingly distant
from his wife and his upper-crust Portland compatriots, he pulled up stakes
and left for Los Gatos, California, to live as a literary bohemian with Sara
Bard Field.

Another of Wood's legal clients was Marie Equi, who came to Oregon
to homestead near The Dalles and graduated from the University of Oregon
medical school in 1903. Brutality during the 1913 strike of women against the
Oregon Packing Company changed Equi from a progressive reformer to a
vehement labor activist and pacifist. Outspoken in opposition to the United
States' entry into World War I, she earned multiple arrests for labor and anti-
war demonstrations and federal prosecution for sedition after an anti-war
speech at the Portland IWW hall in 1918. In a year of anti-radical hysteria,
Wood's defense failed to prevent Equi's conviction and her subsequent sentence to San Quentin. The Portland to which she returned in 1921 to live out
her last thirty years was a far more stolid place than the city of the 1910s—Joe
Hill had been executed in Utah, John Reed had died of typhus in Russia,
C. E. S. Wood was trying to be another Voltaire in his new home in California,
and the acronym associated with dissent in Oregon was now KKK rather than
IWW.

Chapter 5
Modern Times

The problems and opportunities of modern times arrived in Portland with assistance from the Great War in Europe, which turned the city's small shipbuilding business into a major industry. The success of Germany's U-boat campaign in 1916 and 1917 spurred Allied orders from Portland shipbuilders to replace the lost merchant vessels. After the United States entered the war in April 1917, the U.S. Emergency Fleet Corporation made itself the sole customer for nearly a hundred Portland-built steel-hulled and wooden-hulled ships. Shipyard employment climbed to 28,000 at the end of 1918. Foundries, machine shops, and sawmills that supplied materials for the shipbuilders accounted for another 5,000 jobs. Rents rose; newcomers, attracted by wartime jobs, crowded the streets; and workers on three shifts kept the city open 24 hours a day.

Like most other Americans, most Portlanders saw the war effort not only as a chance for a better job but also as a patriotic crusade from which there could be no dissent. Suspicions against immigrants, particularly Germans, ran high. German-born residents had to carry a registration card to work near the waterfront. The Brooklyn neighborhood showed its loyalty by renaming streets, with Frankfurt Street becoming Lafayette and Bismarck becoming Bush, but city council members ignored the Linnton workers, who wanted Germantown Road renamed Libertytown Road.

The U.S. Department of Justice used provisions for internment of enemy aliens to root out members of and sympathizers with the radical Industrial Workers of the World. Clarence Reames, U.S. Attorney for Portland, thought that "every member of the IWW who is an enemy alien as defined by the proclamation of the President" should be interned until the close of the war. Hungarian-born Paul Seidler earned internment by sticking to his Wobbly beliefs even though he agreed that the United States was on the right side in the war. "Socialist tendencies" got Herman Schreiber into more trouble than

George Baker. Four-term mayor George Baker came to politics from a career in the theater, and he knew that success depended as much on making a good impression as on substantial policy ideas. Tall and energetic, he made friends not only by keeping doors open at City Hall but also by once turning out in his shirtsleeves to help neighbors on the east side fight a grass fire that threatened their homes. (Portland City Archives, A 2000-033.83

did his German sympathies. George Zeiger's mistake was to refer to himself as "a citizen of the world."

The loudest voice for "100 percent Americanism" belonged to George Baker, who began his 16-year stint as mayor in 1917, a few weeks after Congress declared war. His campaign promise that "smokestacks will be as numerous as the trees in the forest" continued the tradition of business boosterism. A last-minute revelation that his labor-backed opponent Will Daly had applied for membership in the Socialist party successfully played to growing wartime hysteria. Baker led Liberty Bond rallies and held breakfasts at the Civic Auditorium for each contingent of Oregonians bound for the trenches in France. Throughout the war years, eighty police officers dealt with "outside activities" such as registering aliens, raiding radical organizations, and patrolling railroads and docks to ward off sabotage. Baker also enlisted the police on the side of management and "Americanism" in any labor dispute.

Baker was the most colorful politician in Portland's sometimes bland political history. He stood over six feet tall, weighed in at more than 200 pounds, and easily earned the nomination of the *Oregon Voter* magazine as "the champion loud noise of the Pacific Northwest." Born in The Dalles in 1868, he quit school at the age of nine to shine shoes and sell newspapers on the streets of San Francisco. He came to Portland in 1889 and worked his way up from

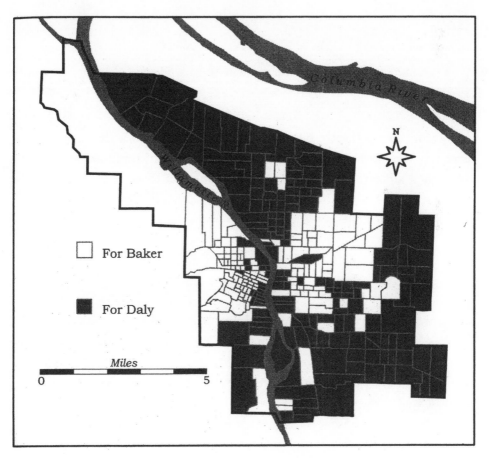

Election map, 1917. Will Daly and George Baker battled down to the wire in the mayoral election of 1917. As this map shows, Baker was the candidate of the business establishment, winning a narrow victory with the support of affluent West Hills precincts and upper-middle-class neighborhoods like Laurelhrust, Grant Park, and Irvington (where he won one precinct 123 to 5). Support for Daly, who supported the cause of organized labor, came from immigrant South Portland and from mixed working-class and lower-white-collar neighborhoods like Sellwood, Woodstock, Overlook, and St. Johns. (Courtesy Robert Johnston)

Southwest First Avenue. Southwest First was the heart of South Portland. Lined with stores and apartments that served Jewish and Italian immigrants and more densely packed than similar east-side streets like Union Avenue (now Martin Luther King Jr. Boulevard), it was the closest that Portland came to the vibrant ethnic shopping districts that were common in larger cities like Philadelphia and Chicago. (Oregon Historical Society, Neg 47144)

the bottom in the theater business. By the first decade of the new century, he owned downtown theaters, managed his own performing stock company, and joined almost every club and organization in town. He served on the city council from 1898 to 1900 and again from 1907 to 1913, representing the downtown voters and vice kings of Ward Four.

Portland's record of intolerance showed no improvement after the Armistice. Fears of international Bolshevism and domestic radicalism intensified in 1919 and 1920. These years also brought severe inflation and high unemployment as shipyards shut down and veterans returned home. A general strike in Seattle early in 1919 and a November shootout in Centralia, Washington, between members of the American Legion and the Wobblies made the Portland establishment more than a little nervous. So did efforts to organize thousands of newly unemployed workers and discharged soldiers into a local equivalent of the worker soviets that were central to the revolution in Russia. Mayor Baker's response was to use the state's new "criminal syndicalism" law, which essentially outlawed radical organizing, to raid the city's IWW offices, shut down meeting halls used by workers, and prohibit banners announcing strikes or workers' meetings from the streets of Portland.

Two years later, seamen in the Pacific Northwest went out on strike against a 25 percent pay cut imposed by the U.S. Shipping Board. Violence came to the Portland waterfront on June 20 when police officers appeared on the docks in plain clothes and confronted pickets. A confused melee of gunfire ended with striker Nestor Varrio dead and his union hauled into court to fight a conspiracy charge. Confrontation on the waterfront occurred again in the fall of 1922, when a thousand longshoremen and members of the Marine Transport Workers (affiliated with the IWW) walked off the job. George Baker put the weight of city government firmly on the side of the Waterfront Employers Association. The city council appropriated $10,000 to fight the "radical revolution." A hundred special police officers descended on the picket lines, arrested all known Wobblies as vagrants, and searched trains entering and leaving Union Station. On the same day that the strike was settled to the satisfaction of the employers, the mayor took credit for averting a revolution.

By the time of the dock strikes, Oregon had also heard the appeal of the "Invisible Empire" of the Ku Klux Klan. As it spread across the South, Middle West, and West in the early 1920s, the Klan appealed to Americans who were disturbed by the rapid pace of social change. The Klan's two million members—factory workers, dentists, store owners, clerks, and craftsmen—were united by their fear that the familiar America was disappearing. The growth of the Klan was in part a reaction against the disturbing times, with their high prices, scarce jobs, and labor agitation. Klansmen blamed these social ills on "outsiders" and "aliens"—particularly blacks, Jews, and Roman Catholic immigrants—and these groups bore the brunt of the Klan's attacks.

The Klan took root in Oregon communities from Tillamook to La Grande. In Portland it found fertile soil in a largely Protestant community that had just experienced five years of turmoil. Kleagle Luther Powell was the chief organizer, and he began to recruit in the summer of 1921. The Exalted Cyclops was Fred Gifford, an electrician who had left his union for a job with the Northwest Electric Company. It is unclear whether George Baker joined the Klan, but he certainly welcomed their support. Compared to those in other parts of the country, Portland's Kluxers committed little vigilante violence and concentrated instead on the voting booth. In May 1922, Klan-backed candidates won 2 of 3 seats on the Multnomah County Commission and 12 of the county's 13 seats in the state legislature.

Portland supplied the victory margin in November for a statewide compulsory public school initiative, which attempted to make all private schools illegal. Backers intended it to attack both elite privilege and Roman Catholic distinctiveness, but the U.S. Supreme Court struck down the law before it went into effect. As in other cities and states, interest in the Klan declined when the novelty of their costumes and rhetoric wore off, and particularly

when people discovered that Klan-backed politicians could be just as venal as
the men they replaced.

Portland's immigrant neighborhoods were reaching their peak in the
same years that many Oregonians were using the Klan to express their un-
certainty about ethnic variety and change. Albina and Brooklyn, Chinatown
and Japantown, Slabtown and South Portland were all neighborhoods where
Portlanders from multiple countries and continents lived, mingled, and sought
to launch their children as successful Americans. Indeed, 1920s prosperity
combined with national restrictions on immigration in 1921 and 1924 meant
that ethnic Portland was changing and dispersing even in the heyday of the
city's stopover neighborhoods.

South Portland is perhaps the best-remembered of these neighborhoods.
Since the turn of the century, its small houses and affordable apartments had
attracted Italians and Jews from Russia and Eastern Europe. Easy access to
downtown made the neighborhood convenient for newcomers with jobs as

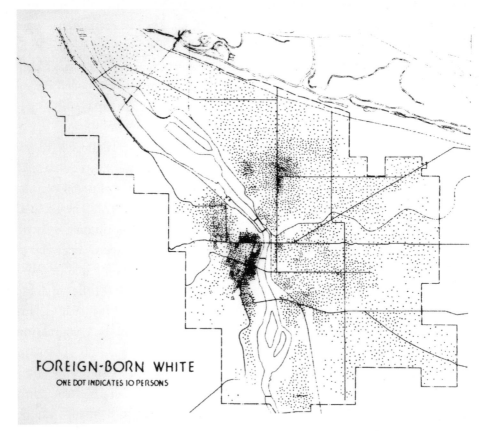

FOREIGN-BORN WHITE
ONE DOT INDICATES 10 PERSONS

Foreign-born population, 1930. The recently formed Portland Planning Commission utilized Depression-
fighting New Deal funds to map the residence of the city's foreign-born residents in 1930. The result showed the
intense concentration of single men from other countries on the fringes of downtown, and clusters of immigrants
in South Portland, Northwest Portland, the Union Avenue and Albina districts, and Brooklyn. (Author's collection)

Montavilla. The Montavilla business district at Southeast Stark and Eightieth, photographed here in 1939, was typical of neighborhood shopping clusters that developed in every quadrant of Portland and its environs, from St. Johns to Multnomah to Sellwood. These early versions of the "twenty-minute neighborhood" desired by 21st century planners usually offered a drug store, grocery, florist, movie theater, variety store, restaurants, and second-floor office space for dentists, insurance agents, lawyers, and other professionals. (Portland City Archives, A 2005.011.630)

construction workers, peddlers, and salesmen. Many immigrants worked in the factories and sawmills along the adjacent waterfront. Others ran small businesses in the commercial core along First Avenue, where streetcars could drop passengers in front of bakeries, drugstores, Italian groceries, kosher markets, meeting rooms for benevolent societies, and theaters showing Italian language movies.

The smallest of small businessmen were the South Portlanders who peddled goods out of horse-drawn wagons. They stabled their horses in neighborhood barns and in Marquam Gulch before it was filled in the 1930s. As one resident recalled, "the gulch in South Portland was the site of horses and wagons of the peddlers. In the morning it was quite a sight to see the horses and wagons stream out of the gulch." Italians were often peddlers of fruits and vegetables, some of which were grown by Italian market gardeners. Jewish peddlers were more often found in the junk trade (we might call it recycling now). Front Avenue was lined with secondhand stores that resold many of the items that the peddlers bought up from backyards.

Much of neighborhood life revolved around churches and synagogues. Jews had founded five synagogues between 1902 and 1916, sometimes buying buildings from Christian congregations (Shaarie Torah took over its building

Swan Island Airport. The Port of Portland built the city's first airport on Swan Island after receiving federal permission to shift the channel of the river from the east side of the island to the west, attaching the "island" to the east bank. Charles Lindbergh inaugurated the airport by landing on September 14, 1927. But the growing size of aircraft, especially the DC-3, made the Swan Island facility obsolete, and air service shifted in 1940 to a larger facility on dragged landfill along the Columbia River. (Portland City Archives, A 2005.055.1407.3)

from Presbyterians, for example). Roman Catholics had St. Lawrence Church and St. Michael's Church. The latter, established in 1901, has a cornerstone which reads CHIESA ITALIANA DI SAN MICHELE ARCANGELO, FABRICATA DELLA COLONIA ITALIANA DI PORTLAND, OREGON.

Children from both groups attended Failing School and Shattuck School. A beautiful new Failing School building (1912) replaced an earlier building that had been built at First and Hooker in 1882. With the extension of Front Avenue still in the future, no concrete barrier separated the new school from the bulk of the neighborhood uphill to its west. Shattuck, built in 1914 and now part of the Portland State University campus, replaced an earlier building at Sixth and Harrison. Less than a mile apart, the two schools were community anchors that sent their graduates to Lincoln High School, housed in its own new building on Southwest Broadway in 1912.

Women from Portland's long-established community of German Jews operated Neighborhood House, one of hundreds of settlement houses that existed throughout the United States in the early 20th century. Beginning with a sewing school and preschool programs for children, the National Council of Jewish Women opened their own building on First Avenue in 1905. Programs grew so rapidly, however, that merchant Ben Selling led a fund-raising effort that financed a new, larger building across from Lair Hill Park, opened in December 1910 and standing a century later. Neighborhood House modeled its programs and activities after Jane Addams's famous Hull House in Chicago. It was a social and cultural center for South Portland, with language classes, vocational training, a kindergarten, a clinic, a well-baby program, and meeting rooms. Open to everyone, it still had a decidedly Jewish orientation. Schoolchildren from the many different synagogues attended Hebrew School on its top floor at the end of long days in public schools.

Even in the 1920s, change was in the air. Completion of the Ross Island Bridge in 1925 took out several blocks for the bridge access ramps and poured traffic onto South Portland's streets. The leading real estate firm of Strong and MacNaughton defined the neighborhood as part of Portland's "breakup zone" where they expected substantial real estate development. "Great changes are now in process," said their newsletter in 1923. "Shrewd investors are . . . planning accordingly." Fifteen years later, the federal Home Owners Loan Corporation published a map of "mortgage risk districts" in Portland (this was one of the notorious "redlining" maps that guided the work of the Federal Housing Administration). South Portland was uniformly colored red, meaning it was "hazardous" to bankers.

The blocks between Burnside Street and Union Station were even more diverse than South Portland. Researchers at Portland State University's Institute for Metropolitan Studies have examined the 1930 census to profile the residents of First, Second, Third, and Fourth between Burnside and Everett. Crowded into cheap hotels and apartments were 1,919 people—1,557 of them single men. A quarter of the total were Japanese, or Chinese, or Filipino. Japanese and Chinese businessmen dominated the streets as tailors, barbers, restaurant owners, and operators of hotels and rooming houses. Both groups also provided most of the neighborhood's families. Chinese households filled some of the buildings and Japanese families filled others nearby—integration by block but not by building. These families shared the neighborhood with single men born in Finland, Sweden, Greece, Germany, and other countries, as well as the United States.

Prosperity during World War I and again in the early 1920s because of a thriving timber industry made it easier for immigrants or their children to move from core neighborhoods to newly built middle-class housing. For example, historian William Toll has traced the movement of successful Jewish shopkeepers and professionals from South Portland and older sections of Northwest Portland to Laurelhurst, Irvington, and Westover Terrace. Many

German and Scandinavian families moved to newer and nicer housing within the northeast sector of the city in the post-World War I era.

These ethnic migrations opened older parts of Albina to a gradually growing African American population. Before World War I, the majority of Portland's 1,000 blacks lived between Burnside, Glisan, Third, and Fourteenth because of the area's convenience to hotel, restaurant, and railroad jobs. Here were black-owned businesses like the Golden West Hotel and Pioneer Billiards Parlor. By the end of the thirties, the census counted 2,000 black residents, with an increasing proportion of families to single men. The growing community organized a branch of the NAACP in 1914 and the Oregon Federation of Colored Women's Clubs in 1917. By 1940, more than half of the city's African Americans lived in Albina, where inexpensive older housing allowed widespread homeownership among stable working-class families and a smattering of businessmen and professionals in a way that paralleled the experience of European immigrants.

The difference between the African American experience and that of the European immigrants was deeply embedded racial discrimination. Realtors urged each other to confine home sales to blacks to Albina. Unions ranging from hotel workers to the longshoremen barred black members. The major hospitals admitted blacks as patients but refused to accept their applications as nurses. Kathleen Hall Bogle summarized the Portland way in a stunning essay for the *Oregonian* in 1937 titled "An American Negro Speaks of Color." She noted the ubiquitous slights, such as high school assemblies where the speaker started out with racist jokes, and the trade schools that had no place for people of color because the other students might object. Contrasting Portland with Los Angeles and Seattle, which had more open labor markets, she described looking for work in Portland:

> I started out buoyant and fresh with the dream of finding an employer without prejudice . . . I visited both large and small stores of all descriptions. I visited the telephone company; both light and power companies. I tried to become an elevator operator in an office building. I answered ads for inexperienced office help. In all these places where vacancies occurred I was told there was nothing about me in my disfavor, except the color of my skin.

Most Portlanders in the roaring twenties were more interested in enjoying their new automobiles and the products of postwar production than thinking about racial discrimination. When the United States entered World

War I, there was one automobile in Multnomah County for every 13 residents. The ratio increased to one automobile for every 5 residents in 1925 and one for every 3.7 residents by 1929. Automobiles were big business. At the end of the 1920s there were eighty dealers in the first "automobile rows" along North Broadway, between Tenth and Twenty-First west of downtown, and on the near east side. Portland residents spent as much on automobiles as they did on food, and 8,000 depended directly on automobiles for their jobs.

As early as 1913, a hundred business and professional men had formed a kind of posse of automobilists known as the "Flying Squadron," roaming town in their own cars to enforce 10- and 15-mile-per-hour speed limits and generally trying to maintain order in the streets. The first comprehensive city code for motorists and pedestrians came in 1914. The police department set up an auto theft bureau in 1920 and a "speed squad" in 1922. Congestion downtown became a special headache as thousands of cars clogged narrow streets, fought streetcars for the right-of-way, and parked wherever they pleased. The twenties brought the first no-parking zones and the first automatic signals, though as late as 1931, only a quarter of downtown intersections had the two-color lights that announced their change from green to red with a clanging bell.

Marquam Hill Medical Complex. In 1919 the University of Oregon Medical School moved from Northwest Portland to a then bucolic location on Marquam Hill. The driving force was Kenneth A. J. Mackenzie, dean of the school and, in Kimbark MacColl's words, a man of "high achievement motivation" who secured 22 acres from the Union Pacific Railroad and an additional 88 acres from *Oregon Journal* publisher C. S. Jackson. Once the Medical School began to attract adjacent hospitals in the 1920s, including this Veteran's Administration Hospital, the inertia of steel and stone has kept replacement and expansion buildings on the same hilltops ever since. (Portland City Archives, A 2004-002.71)

St. Johns Bridge construction. The St. Johns Bridge, opened in 1931, was Portland's first suspension span, allowing it to arc high above the river from high point to high point and avoid the necessity of a lift or drawbridge component. Built for what was then a whopping pricetag of $4 million after vociferous lobbying by the Peninsula Bridge Committee, it used up most of Multnomah County's bonding capacity at the onset of the Depression even though it came in under budget. Beautiful as it was, it carried no more than 3 percent of cross-river traffic and preempted construction of a more-needed span closer to the center of industry until the Fremont Bridge was built forty years later. (Portland City Archives, 2012.30)

"Autoists" demanded wide, hard-surfaced roads and new bridges. The Interstate Bridge across the Columbia opened in 1917, connecting Portland to Vancouver over a recently improved and appropriately renamed Interstate Avenue. By 1924, motorists could follow the paved Pacific Highway from downtown Portland across the Broadway and Interstate bridges all the way to Tacoma and Seattle. The city spent millions widening east and west Burnside, Sandy Boulevard, Union Avenue, 82nd Avenue, and other arterial streets. Multnomah County put millions more into reconstructing the Burnside Bridge and building the Ross Island Bridge. The Sellwood Bridge, built in 1925, and the St. Johns Bridge, built in 1931, were harder to justify to taxpayers in terms of traffic, but they did help to tie the two historically isolated neighborhoods for which they were named more closely to the rest of the city.

Automobiles and paved streets made it feasible to develop areas that had been inconvenient for streetcar riders. A building boom in the 1920s brought Portland 25,000 new houses. Builders and buyers also filled in vacant lots in east-side neighborhoods such as Eastmoreland, Grant Park, Mount Tabor, and Concordia, all of which were located three to six miles from the center of town. New high schools—Cleveland, Roosevelt, Grant—served the growing neighborhoods and provided a focus for community identity.

Automobiles also opened the previously inaccessible West Hills, for they could climb steep slopes that stymied streetcars. Owners of new houses in Westover, Arlington Heights, Portland Heights, and Council Crest could overlook the older Victorian city with the assurance that they had achieved economic success. Many of these homes were built in an emerging regional style that ignored "period" references in favor of natural wood and cedar shingles that blended architectural design with the natural setting. Architects John Yeon and Pietro Belluschi expanded this approach with innovative designs during the 1930s and 1940s. Yeon based his Watzek House on Oregon vernacular forms, while Belluschi's Joss House spotlighted local materials with unfinished cedar paneling and spruce siding. According to historian George McMath, Belluschi's Jennings-Sutor House of 1938 had all the characteristics of contemporary design with its "concern for the setting and integration of landscaping, the open functional plan, the broad sheltering pitched roof, and the use of naturally finished native woods."

New neighborhoods and more automobiles also meant commercial strips along major streets. Eighty-second Avenue changed from a country road to a string of stores and gas stations between 1920 and 1940. The new Barbur Boulevard, built on an unused Southern Pacific railroad right-of-way in the early 1930s, avoided the same fate through protective zoning. Sandy Boulevard became the shrieking symbol of an automobile city. Architect Al Staehli has described it as "a linear Disneyland of buildings which were also the symbols of their function. Stucco shoes for shoe shops, gas pumps tucked under mushroom canopies, giant milk bottles crowding a dairy, jug taverns, and the grinning black-face entrance of the Coon Chicken Inn [now mercifully vanished] provided a series of visual exclamation points."

Zoning took on the larger function of protecting residential neighborhoods against the intrusion of businesses, apartment houses, and gas stations. George Baker and his establishment allies first proposed land-use zoning in 1919 and 1920 as a response to the wartime boom and its uncontrolled growth. Voters in 1920 narrowly rejected the plan, with most working-class neighborhoods opposed and upper-middle-class areas in favor. Banker John C. Ainsworth had argued that zoning would "harmonize the property interest of owners and the health, safety and convenience of the public," but many small property holders were suspicious of any restriction on development rights. A second try succeeded in 1924. The simple code, written jointly by the Planning Commission and Realty Board, divided the city into four zones—one was limited to single-family houses; another allowed apartments; a third allowed businesses; and a final industrial zone allowed virtually anything else.

With the help of the automobile, Portland carried on its intense love affair with the outdoors. One of the community's most enduring accomplishments was the Columbia River Highway, opened between Troutdale and Hood River in 1915 and completed all the way to The Dalles in 1922. Engineer Sam Lancaster designed a road that complemented and blended with the spectacular landscape of the Columbia Gorge, achieving his aim "to find the beauty spots, or those points where the most beautiful things along the line might be seen to the best advantage, and if possible to locate the road in such a way as to reach them." The highway was built jointly by Multnomah County and the state, with essential help from millionaire lumbermen Simon Benson and John Yeon. The Portland City Directory called the highway "America's newest and greatest pathway for the recreationist." Hotels, auto camps, and restaurants sprang up in the Gorge towns, and the U.S. Forest Service opened a campground at Eagle Creek and set aside its first "Recreation Reserve" of 14,000 acres. Completion of a paved road to Tillamook and Seaside and a highway loop around Mount Hood in the 1920s brought the outdoors even closer to mobile Portlanders.

Portland slid inexorably from good times to bad after 1929. The city as a whole escaped the worst ravages that the Great Depression brought to the industrial cities of the East and the farms of the South, but local business grew worse and worse over four very long years. The Depression cut the city's exports and banking activity by more than half. The value of new construction in 1933 and again in 1934 was scarcely over $2 million—6 percent of the 1925 record. Business failures peaked in 1932, but the worst was still to come for retailers. Thousands of families dug up their backyards for vegetable gardens and canceled their telephone service to save a few dollars a month. Theater owners went broke for lack of customers despite drawings and giveaways. Two of every three small businesses were behind on their property taxes by 1933.

When Franklin D. Roosevelt took office, the Portland Public Employment Bureau listed 24,000 unemployed householders. Welfare payments, though inadequate, helped to support 9,100 families. From May 1932 through the end of the year, the City of Portland sold $845,000 in bonds to fund work relief projects. Eighteen thousand men signed up for jobs, and 4,000 actually went to work on park and street improvements. In March 1933, when the money ran out, the city continued the program by paying the workers with

Burnside before and after widening. Like many U.S. cities, Portland in the 1920s and 1930s began to devote increasing amounts of land to space-hungry automobiles. Looking west past the intersection of West Burnside and Broadway, these pictures show Burnside before and after widening in the 1930s. Workers demolished some buildings; they sliced the fronts off others and reattached the facades twenty feet back. (Portland City Archives, A 2011-022.6 and A 1999-044.257)

scrip—formal IOUs that 2,500 merchants agreed to accept as cash, with the promise that the city would later redeem the scrip at full value.

Besides the implementation of public jobs programs, the 1930s were a time when communities helped themselves out of necessity. The Catholic

Public Market. In 1936, Portland replaced an unkempt set of market stalls along Yamhill Street with a new Public Market Building that stretched for two blocks between Front Street and the new sea wall. Despite its rather stylish art deco look, it was an instant white elephant (or beached white whale), used by the military during World War II and then by the *Oregon Journal* before it was demolished in 1969. (Arnold Rothstein, Library of Congress)

Women's League found temporary jobs for 500 women and girls in 1932 and gave short-term assistance to 500 others. The members of the Council of Jewish Women opened a bake shop to provide supplemental employment for poorer residents of South Portland. The city's most prestigious families rallied around the Portland Symphony Society with contributions and memberships to keep the musicians playing in the 1931–32 season.

The citywide Council of Social Agencies organized ten neighborhood councils in 1934 to coordinate services for children and fight juvenile delinquency. By the late 1930s many of the councils had expanded their concerns to the larger issue of neighborhood livability and to problems such as housing, health, and city services. These groups were the predecessors for Portland's neighborhood associations, which began to develop in the 1960s.

Portlanders who went unassisted by public and private relief agencies often ended up in one of the city's "Hoovervilles"—shantytowns for the homeless.

The biggest of these stretched along the slopes of Sullivan's Gulch from the Union and Grand avenue overpasses out to Twenty-First Avenue. Hundreds of men lived in self-built shacks made with scrounged lumber, scraps from construction sites, and liberated tar paper. Much like a frontier mining camp, the settlement had its own rules and its own informal leadership. There were other squatter settlements at Ross Island and on the filled site of Guild's Lake.

The Depression polarized Portland politics. A wide spectrum of views and bitter arguments replaced the unadventurous "hail-fellow-well-met" city council of the 1920s. At one extreme was the Red-baiting councilman J. E. Bennett, described even by the conservative *Oregon Voter* as contentious and obnoxious. At the other extreme was Councilman Ralph Clyde, a strong and persistent advocate for municipal ownership of electric utilities. Joseph Carson, mayor from 1933 to 1940, was a states' rights Democrat who worked hard to keep the New Deal out of Portland. He was a special friend of the private utilities and an enemy of organized labor. Proposals for new government programs such as public housing often lost, three votes to two, with future mayor Earl Riley joining Carson and Bennett in opposition. The liberal Ralph Clyde was joined in the minority by architect Ormond Bean, who would serve on the city council from 1933 to 1939 and again from 1948 to 1966.

Not just the city council but the entire community split over the Longshore strike of 1934, one of the most bitter labor-management battles in Portland's history. Since the strike of 1922, which the workers had lost, Portland's docks had been run by waterfront employers. In the fall of 1933, in response to deteriorating working conditions and wage cuts, the International Longshoremen's Association organized a single local for the entire Pacific coast. A coastwise strike started on May 9, 1934, and closed down the port. Before it was over, 82 days later, the strike had directly involved 3,000 waterfront workers and idled another 15,000 Portlanders in trade-dependent jobs. The central issue was the balance of power on the docks, with the strikers demanding employer recognition and union control of hiring halls.

The Portland police were in a pivotal position between the antagonists. In the first weeks of the strike, they allowed pickets to run strikebreakers off the docks and attack the shipping company security forces. Strikers raided one ship—the *Admiral Evans*—that was moored near the Steel Bridge as a floating hotel for strikebreakers, cutting it loose to drift against the Broadway Bridge. By early summer, Mayor Carson gave in to demands from the business community and enlisted the city on the side of waterfront employers. July 5, 1934, became known as "Bloody Thursday," when a concerted effort to break the strike in all the Pacific ports led to several deaths in other cities and a number of arrests in Portland. Senator Robert Wagner of New York arrived on July 12 as a special representative of President Roosevelt, who was scheduled to visit the site of Bonneville Dam in August. Wagner's mission was to settle the strike before Roosevelt steamed into Portland harbor in the U.S.S. *Houston*. Company guards shot at Wagner's car when he tried to visit Terminal 4, perhaps without knowing who he was. Fortunately, the only injury was to the reputation of Portland. This incident, plus the threat of delaying the president's visit, gave Wagner leverage to force employers to agree to arbitration. Portland's establishment worked out the painful details in a secret meeting at the Arlington Club, tacitly recognizing the union by agreeing to submit the dispute to arbitration. The victorious longshoremen went back to work on July 31, with the foundation laid for the emergence of the International Longshore and Warehouse Union later in the decade.

As Portland's business community knew well, the best chance for a new Portland during the troubled years of the Depression was the development of cheap hydroelectric power. From Franklin D. Roosevelt's visit to dedicate the site in August 1934 to its official completion in September 1937, Portlanders on weekend excursions could watch the great bulk of Bonneville Dam rise across the channel of the Columbia 40 miles east of the city. Construction provided paychecks for 5,000 workers and held out the possibility of transforming Portland into what FDR described as "a vast city of whirling machinery."

One benefit of hydroelectric power was the promise of reducing the pall of wood smoke that hung over the city each winter. Portlanders in the 1920s and 1930s heated their houses with wood. Some fed their furnaces with basements full of sawdust. Others used cordwood that they piled up each fall on front parking strips. Mill workers near the Northwest waterfront hauled home waste wood and the slabs that were discarded as saws squared logs into lumber—hence the name "Slabtown" for their neighborhood. The smoke grew worse in the 1930s when huge forest fires ravaged the Coast Range. Author Beverly Cleary recalled her first day at Grant High School in 1933, "when smoke from forest fires dimmed the atmosphere, the sun was a sullen orange ball, and ash drifted over the City."

The Willamette River itself could be as dirty as the air overhead. Towns upriver from Portland poured sewage into the river. So did paper mills and food-processing plants, whose organic waste sucked oxygen out of the water as it decayed and turned the river into a killing zone for fish. The Portland City Club called the river "filthy and ugly" in 1927. Conservation organizations including the Izaak Walton League and Oregon Wildlife Federation placed an anti-pollution measure on the 1938 ballot. The voters created the Oregon

Kids on 23rd Avenue. Children on Northwest 23rd Avenue, perhaps dressed up for the Rose Festival. The date is likely the 1920s, with the old Good Samaritan Hospital building poking over rooftops in the background. (Gholston Collection)

State Sanitary Authority (predecessor of the Department of Environmental Quality) as a first step toward Willamette River cleanup, although the City of Portland itself was a major polluter that dragged its feet on remedial measures.

New Deal liberals in Oregon hoped for an independent Columbia Valley Authority that would distribute the new hydroelectrically generated power at equal rates throughout the Northwest. But the Portland Chamber of Commerce, Mayor Carson, and a procession of businessmen argued that Bonneville's electricity should be available at lower rates within a 50-mile radius of the turbines. A congressional compromise created the Bonneville Power Administration (BPA) to market electricity from Grand Coulee Dam as well as Bonneville over a grid connecting Portland, Spokane, and Seattle-Tacoma.

The key decisions involving Bonneville came in 1940. First, voters in the May primary turned down the creation of a public utility district, which would have been empowered to buy out Northwest Electric (now Pacific Power) and Portland Electric Power (now Portland General Electric). As a result, private utilities remained the intermediaries that bought hydro power from the BPA and retailed it to consumers. Second, the BPA offered to sell cheap energy directly to major industries to encourage economic development. In January, Alcoa Aluminum signed the first direct contract for its new aluminum reduction plant in Vancouver. By the following year, Bonneville electricity was also powering federally owned aluminum operations at Troutdale and at Longview, Washington. Within a decade, the dam had made electro-chemical and electro-metallurgical industries the leading manufacturing sector in the greater Portland region.

The practicalities of power policy (and politics) defined one direction for a post-Depression Oregon. Portlanders who wanted other choices could listen to Lewis Mumford, the nation's leading writer on urban planning, who visited in the summer of 1938. In a speech to the City Club and in a pamphlet called "Regional Planning in the Northwest," Mumford called for active yet careful regional planning. He advised Portland to stabilize its population to allow time to clean up thousands of unfit houses, overcrowded apartments, and slum hotels. He also suggested decentralizing new industry into satellite towns whose carefully chosen locations and reliance on electricity would protect the natural environment.

Mumford set his suggestions within an even broader challenge to Portland's abiding conservatism: "I have seen nothing so tempting as a home for man as this Oregon country . . . and I am going to ask you a question which you may not like. Are you good enough to have this country in your possession? Have you got enough intelligence, imagination, and cooperation among you to make best use of these opportunities? . . . In providing for new developments you have an opportunity here to do a job of city planning like nowhere else in the world." In fact, it took another thirty years of boom, bust, and business as usual before Portland and Oregon came to agreement on an agenda for the future. Not until the administration of Governor Tom McCall in the early 1970s would the sort of regional planning that Mumford called for attract the necessary combination of political leadership and popular support.

In the meanwhile, Portland in the 1930s was two cities side by side. Militant union members, skid-road workers, and the periodically unemployed were the labor force that kept Portland factories and docks in motion as they had since the early years of the century. Middle-class visitors saw a different city—solid, sober, politically and socially conventional. They found it "prudent and placid" in the words of journalist Freeman Tilden in 1931, more sympathetic with the ideas of Calvin Coolidge than Franklin Roosevelt. Five years later, Ernie Pyle tried to capture the essence of a city that was simultaneously modest, comfortable, and conservative:

> Portland is a place, they say, where money doesn't get you anywhere
> socially. I asked what *does* get you somewhere—what, in other
> words, was the standard for social admittance in Portland. They

thought and they thought. They finally decided that the standard was merely the ability to contribute something—usually agreeableness and interest. It was settled by "down Easters" who came around the Horn. They made the money and became the backbone. They're still the backbone and the pacesetters of Portland thought. But they have somehow mixed their New England soundness with a capacity for living the freer, milder Northwest way, and it makes for a pretty high-class combination.

Guild's Lake war housing. Sprawling across filled land that stretched along St. Helen's Road and included the former site of the 1905 Lewis and Clark Exposition, Guild's Lake Courts were home for roughly 10,000 war workers and their families in 2,606 housing units. Shown here in 1946, these provided affordable postwar housing for single-parent families and African Americans with few other options, and it temporarily took in people displaced by the Vanport Flood in 1948. The last residents left in 1952, as industrial uses claimed the location with its river and railroad lines. (Photo by Hugh Ackroyd, courtesy Thomas Robinson)

Chapter 6
The War and After

World War II brought more excitement to Portland than anything since the great Exposition. In the language of city officials who worried about problems of the home front, the Portland metropolis was a "congested war production area." But in terms of the pace of daily life, it was a boom town—another Leadville or Dawson City with defense contracts in place of gold and silver mines.

Newfound prosperity came from a single industry—shipbuilding. The first federal orders for new ships went to the Commercial Iron Company, the Albina Shipyard, and Albina Iron and Steel in 1940 and 1941. Industrialist Henry Kaiser of California, fresh from helping to build Boulder and Grand Coulee dams, also opened the huge Oregon Shipbuilding Company at St. Johns in 1941. His Swan Island and Vancouver yards went into production two months after Pearl Harbor.

At the peak of wartime production in 1943 and 1944, metropolitan Portland counted 140,000 defense workers. Federal contracts totaled $2.4 billion for more than a thousand oceangoing ships. The record-breaker for construction time was a Liberty ship launched on September 23, 1942, less than 11 days after workers laid down its keel.

The boom brought thousands of new faces to Portland. The Kaiser yards placed help-wanted ads in 11 states. The response nearly emptied the rest of Oregon, and drew the unemployed from small towns in Idaho and Montana. Workers arrived on chartered trains from the East Coast. The Portland-area population grew from 501,000 to 661,000 between 1940 and 1944. One could safely assume, in the war years, that every third person standing in line for the bus or a double feature was new to town.

Phenomenal growth brought unprecedented problems for local governments. The job explosion on the north side of the city strained public transportation in an era of gasoline and tire rationing. Two hundred new buses, 150 trucks, and ferry service across the Willamette to Swan Island were scarcely enough to keep up with the demand. The tens of thousands of shipyard workers, many of whom were unmarried or without their families, also had money for liquor, gambling, and prostitution. While the circulation of books from the public library dropped, the pari-mutuel handle at the dog tracks skyrocketed. A cleanup drive in 1942 swept out the red-light district north of Burnside. Gamblers, however, simply moved their shops to the side streets, and prostitution dispersed but didn't disappear. City officials complained that it was difficult to protect public safety when the military services had taken nearly half of the city's police officers and firefighters.

With a seemingly endless demand for workers, the Portland and Vancouver shipyards provided high-paying jobs for tens of thousands of Portland women. By the end of 1943, 20,500 women made up a quarter of the Kaiser workforce. One out of three of these women filled the sorts of office jobs that were already open to women, but hundreds of others who had recently graduated from training classes at Benson High filled jobs as electricians, painters, machinists, and pipefitters. Women at Swan Island, Kaiser-Vancouver, Commercial Ironworks, Willamette Iron and Steel, and smaller firms were tool checkers, shipfitters, warehouse clerks, and shipwright helpers. More than 5,000 earned what was then an impressive $1.20 per hour as welders. Welder Ree Adkins later remembered that "in all this kind of work, the women and men were paid the same . . . there didn't seem to be a speck of jealousy. The men did the same things that we did." Another woman recalled of herself and a friend, "We both had to work, we both had children, so we became welders, and if I might say so, damn good ones."

Newly employed mothers relied on a quickly devised child care system made possible by federal subsidies to the schools, to nonprofit agencies, and to employers. Kaiser's special Women's Services Department operated child care centers on round-the-clock shifts synchronized with those of the shipyards and provided take-out meals that could be ordered ahead of time and picked up by busy wives on their way home.

By the time the United States entered the war, few observers thought Portland would be able to cope with its growth. Long-time residents regarded their new neighbors with mixed emotions—puzzlement, hostility, and often jealousy of their relatively high wages. "The people of Portland make it clear that an Arkie or Okie is the most undesirable person on earth," complained one refugee from the dust bowl. Some county election officials thought that migrants from the South were "not fit to vote." A writer for *Fortune* magazine

Day Shifters through for the day, Oregon Shipbuilding Corporation

Shipyards. Quitting time for day-shift workers at Henry Kaiser's Oregon Shipbuilding facility. The throng includes some of the thousands of women who worked in the shipyards, including a few wearing their hard hats for the trip home. (Gholston Collection)

summed it up: "Portland neither likes nor knows how to accommodate its Virginia City atmosphere."

On the positive side, the *Oregonian* and *Oregon Journal* worked to reduce social tension by portraying newcomers as hardworking pioneers who had trekked westward to make new homes. News photos showed newcomers cultivating vegetable gardens outside their trailer homes and stories talked about hardworking tenants making the best of muddy housing projects like modern homesteaders. Even the Portland Art Museum got into the act, working with Kaiser to mount a widely applauded "Ships for Victory" exhibit that might have been more likely in a museum of science and industry than in an insecure and aspiring art museum.

Portland's actual record included a mixture of accomplishments and missed opportunities. On the positive side, the city stepped up to meet the immediate emergency and managed to house 150,000 extra people. But at the same time, it emerged from the war with a legacy of problems, and its leaders often took the easy route by treating only the short-range symptoms.

Responses to the severe housing crunch represented both aspects of Portland's wartime experience. As industry began to mobilize during 1941, the City Planning Commission tried to meet housing needs with Columbia Villa, Portland's first public housing project, which offered newcomers 400 apartments near the shipyards on North Woolsey Avenue. Although its

Guild's Lake Courts. Guild's Lake Courts had enough children to fill five community centers and its own public school, plus spillover to other Portland schools. All of the children in this "clean-up day" picture are white, but African Americans participated in volunteer fire brigades and in the racially integrated Junior Police Patrol. (Portland City Archives, A 2005-025.228)

low-rise design and wide lawns pleased architects, it scarcely made a dent in the ongoing demand.

The focus shifted from permanent to temporary housing when the city council created the Housing Authority of Portland as an emergency measure within days after the attack on Pearl Harbor. The council picked a realtor, a banker, an apartment owner, and a union leader to lead the new agency. Their goal was not to use public housing to shape a more efficient or pleasant city, but to build the minimum number of necessary units, which could be torn down after the war.

The housing crisis peaked in the summer of 1942, when federal officials projected the need for 30,000 additional rooms and apartments. Edgar Kaiser, managing his father's enterprises in Portland, took direct action. At a closed-door meeting in August, he signed a contract with the United States Maritime Commission for an immense 6,000-unit housing development (soon increased to 10,000 units). To the astonishment of city officials, Kaiser broke ground soon after Labor Day. Nearly 5,000 construction workers descended on one square mile of Columbia River floodplain outside the Portland city limits—the present site of Delta Park—to begin construction of 700 identical buildings. Less than six months later, on December 12, 1942, the first tenants moved into the instant community of Vanport.

Vanporters paid a price for hasty development. Though what observers called the "miracle city" had been built from a single blueprint, Housing Authority director Harry Freeman vehemently denied that it was a "planned city," which would have been anathema in conservative Portland. Recognizing the antipathy of Portland's business leaders to anything that reminded them of government planning through New Deal programs, Freeman insisted that Vanport "grew on paper and on the ground as many other American cities have grown." With a population that exceeded 40,000 by 1944, Vanport was the nation's largest housing project and was billed as the second largest "city" in Oregon. No amount of promotion, however, could conceal the reality of its dull gray buildings awash in a sea of winter mud.

The Housing Authority assumed responsibility for maintaining public safety and providing the minimum of social services, such as schools and recreation. The former city manager of Oregon City took on the job of community manager. Although members of the social-work staff tried to build community cohesion through tenant councils, the Authority ignored them more often than not. It was equally cautious about a proposal for a community newspaper. The result of this general disinterest was that nothing in either the development's community life or its cracker-box design could convince residents that Vanport was anything more than a huge tourist camp.

Portland's other huge war housing project, Guild's Lake Courts, made much less of an impression on the community's memory. It was big, with 8,000 white residents and 2,000 African Americans, but not as big as Vanport. Built on filled land at the site of the 1905 Exposition, it disappeared piece by piece between 1945 and 1951 rather than vanishing in a single disastrous day, as Vanport would. Nevertheless, it was a vital temporary neighborhood with its own schools, community centers, and gradations of status (a few households enjoyed electric kitchens but most made do with wood-burning stoves). It was a great place for children, who could volunteer to help the war effort or explore the nearby river and hills when they were out of school. It was also meant to be temporary, for the area had long been planned to turn into what it is today—the Northwest Industrial District.

Guild's Lake Courts and Vanport reconfirmed racial segregation as a fact of Portland life. The city's African American population had increased from 2,100 to 15,000 during the war and presented Portlanders with a new challenge that they largely failed to meet. During 1943, when the African American migration had reached significant proportions, the weekly *People's Observer* chronicled racial incidents on the city buses, harassment by the police, and conflict with the segregated Boilermakers Union. City officials worried about

Vanport flood. In 1948, Vanport still counted 18,500 people, many of them African Americans who found it difficult to secure other housing. It gained a whispered reputation for welfare clients and crime, and Mayor Earl Riley called it a "municipal monstrosity." The Columbia River intervened on Memorial Day, May 30, 1948. Swollen by weeks of heavy rain, the water breached the Northern Pacific Railway embankment at 4:17 p.m. and backfilled the low-lying community. (Portland City Archives, A 2004-002.867)

the possibility of "Detroit incidents," referring to racial riots in the Motor City in 1942 and 1943. Plans to set up a segregated USO in northeast Portland were an additional slap in the face to many African Americans.

Housing lay at the heart of the racial tensions. In 1942, white workers complained about sharing shipyard dormitories with African Americans. For both single black men and black families, little private housing was available outside the Albina neighborhood in near Northeast Portland. Neighborhood groups raised loud protests at every rumor of African Americans moving into their areas. Former City Commissioner J. E. Bennett even went so far as to suggest that Kaiser stop hiring black workers. Mayor Earl Riley agreed in private that the racial migration threatened Portland's "regular way of life."

During the course of the war, the African American population of Albina rose from 2,000 to 3,000, but most of the newcomers found homes in Portland and Vancouver defense housing projects, where they were effectively segregated from the majority of Portlanders. The Housing Authority blandly denied a policy of discrimination, but it carefully steered the thousands of African Americans into certain sections and buildings. At Guild's Lake, where black housing was at the far northern end, some white residents were unaware that

Vanport flood. Residents had 35 minutes to escape the Vanport flood waters. The rising water tumbled automobiles and swirled wooden apartment buildings off their foundations like toy boats, killing 15 residents. (Photo by Allan deLay, courtesy Thomas Robinson)

any African Americans lived there. Vanport's African American families sent their children to integrated schools, but the ill or injured found treatment at a segregated hospital. The Multnomah County sheriff's office triggered a series of nasty confrontations when it tried to prevent racial mixing at recreation centers.

By V-J Day, Vanport housed a largely segregated population of 6,000 African Americans in addition to thousands of white veterans and their families, who occupied temporary quarters while the civilian housing market hurried to meet their needs. Vanport provided Portland a convenient district where African Americans could be isolated from the rest of the city, until the surging waters of the Columbia River wiped out the instant city on May 30, 1948, and forced its African American residents to crowd into Albina.

The city was not welcoming. The Egyptian Theater along Union Avenue (now Martin Luther King Jr. Boulevard) reserved its main floor for white customers even though it was located in walking distance from many the homes of black families. The city council passed a nondiscrimination ordinance for public accommodations in 1950, but the voters repealed it. As late as 1955, the Portland Realty Board acknowledged that its 360 members followed a "code of ethics which prohibits them from selling houses in white districts without the consent of the neighbors."

Vanport protest. Vanport flood refugees picket City Hall a month after the flood to demand permanent low-cost housing. The sign in the center refers to President's Truman's recent request for military and economic aid to Greece and Turkey to allow their governments to combat pressure from the USSR. The flood also sparked unfounded but persistent rumors in the African American community that the Housing Authority had deliberately withheld warnings about the flood and the city had concealed a much higher death toll. (Gholston Collection)

Vanport's postwar record had been mixed. Many established Portlanders shuddered at its undeserved reputation for crime and were quietly relieved when the brown floodwaters tore its buildings from their foundations and swirled them into a logjam of broken memories. For many demobilized veterans, however, the college-level courses offered at the Vanport Extension Center by the Oregon State Board of Higher Education opened the door to new opportunities. When the classes were relocated to the old Lincoln High School building in downtown Portland in 1952, after a stopover at the decommissioned Oregon Shipyards site, the city was well on its way to gaining its own public university. The legislature recognized it as Portland State College in 1955.

Portlanders greeted the end of the war with an immense sigh of relief. The *Oregonian* noted in 1945 that a few younger entrepreneurs were working diligently at industrial development, but that older and established businessmen were shrugging off their aggressive promotional efforts with the argument that Portland and its hinterland lacked the customers to attract manufacturing. Writing two years later in the *Saturday Evening Post*, journalist Richard Neuberger argued that "most Portlanders, if polled by Doctor Gallup, would probably say they want their city to go on being the sort of place it has always been. This means a slow and easygoing trading center, with

lumber its principal shipment and scenery the great nonexportable resource."
Having experienced the fever of the shipbuilding boom, old residents were
grateful that the economic and social temperature of their city was dropping
back down to normal. Neuberger—a liberal Democrat who would later be
elected to the United States Senate—made the observation that everything in
Portland was slowing down; from the speed of its traffic to its search for new
jobs to replace wartime shipbuilding.

In the first decade after the war, Portland voters consistently turned
down spending measures that would have improved the quality of life. Voters did approve $24 million in bonds in May 1944 to fund highway, sewer,
dock, and school projects called for by city planner Robert Moses in a special
report titled *Portland Improvement.* But they soon followed by rejecting tax
increases or bond measures for a civic center, a war memorial, sewer improvements, and urban redevelopment. Voters also turned down a forty-hour
work week and pay increases for city employees. They rejected a proposal
to establish low-income housing in 1950 and bond issues for the zoo and
symphony in 1952. Portlanders carefully filled school board positions with
realtors who could be trusted to keep property taxes low. A climax of sorts
to this conservative era came in the spring of 1958, when Portlanders handed
a stinging defeat to proposals for public transit funding and for a ten-year
capital improvements program.

The city did flirt with political change in 1948. Even during his wartime
vice crackdown, Mayor Earl Riley had complained that it made more sense
to regulate illegitimate businesses than to try to legislate human nature. As he
wrote a constituent in 1945, "There is, no doubt, some gambling going on in
Portland. There always has been and, to be frank with you, there always will
be." However, it became apparent to concerned citizens soon after the war
that many law enforcement officials were living well beyond their salaries.
Riley's new police chief was Lee Jenkins, an old friend who had served 16
years in the same position for George Baker and who was unlikely to reform
the department. In January 1948, the nationally respected criminal justice
consultant August Vollmer, whom Riley had hired under pressure, found
the Portland police to be demoralized and mismanaged. A month later, the
City Club counted 11 brothels and 10 gambling dens that operated openly in
the old red-light district north of Burnside. Systematic payoffs to the police
reportedly made their way to a special safe in the mayor's office.

Finance Commissioner Dorothy McCullough Lee stepped forward to
challenge Riley in the May 1948 primary election when it looked as if the
downtown establishment was willing to go along with business as usual. After

her victory and inauguration as mayor in 1949, Lee reinvigorated the vice
squad and attacked the prevalence of gambling. The campaign, it turned out,
annoyed not only the underworld but also the supposedly respectable American Legion and the Multnomah Athletic Club, where slot machine revenues
helped keep dues low.

Mayor Lee also tried for fundamental reform of Portland's governmen-
tal structure. Asserting that rapid growth required a more efficient municipal
administration, she appointed businessmen and civic leaders to a Committee
on Municipal Reorganization. However, the city council balked at placing a
city manager charter, recommended by the mayor's committee, on the ballot,
as individual commissioners defended their independent domains. Lacking
the support of the daily papers, which argued that Portland enjoyed quite
adequate, if somewhat unwieldy, government, the city manager advocates
failed to gather enough signatures for their petitions to place the proposal on
the ballot.

In both cases, Dorothy Lee was a serious, socially conservative reformer
who found it hard to gain traction with Portland's "old boys" business elite.
Her political goals were not drastically different from those of rising politicians like Barry Goldwater in Phoenix, but the newspapers preferred to talk
about her hats and outfits instead of her ideas. Colleagues on the city council
thought they knew better than she did—especially Public Works Commissioner William Bowes (1939–69), who modeled himself on Robert Moses
and snorted at what he considered the disastrous notions of Lee and other
reformers. The movers and shakers got together at the all-male Arlington
Club and similar locations rather than engage in public debates.

The next four years marked a low point in municipal affairs. Journalist
Phil Stanford sets the scene: "It was business as usual again in the Rose City.
As it had been for decades, the well-oiled rackets machine was now free to
operate, more or less openly, under the protection of the city government. At
the head of the new administration was Fred Peterson [Portland's mayor from
1953 to 1956]. If he didn't understand the payoff system, no one did." The
wild card in the mid-1950s was the Teamsters Union, operating out of Seattle
under Dave Beck, flush with money from new members, and led by people
looking for shady ways to get rich. The Teamsters muscled in on Portland's
liquor trade and its pinball, punchboard, and slot machine operations and
used their control of deliveries to muzzle local business resistance. Multnomah County District Attorney William Langley was happy to be bought
off for $2,000 a month. A standoff between two Republican governors and
the Democratic attorney general stymied action at the state level.

Dorothy Lee. The first woman to serve as mayor of Portland, Dorothy Lee was a progressive and somewhat straitlaced reformer at a time when Portland's establishment preferred to let a little vice and corruption slide by. Here she inspects a traffic signal designed to help sightless pedestrians cross 82nd Avenue. (Portland City Archives, A 2005-001.1131)

In 1956, a falling out among crooks let *Oregonian* reporters Wallace Turner and William Lambert research a month-long series about crime and corruption that broke on April 19. A state-directed grand jury indicted Langley, Police Chief James Purcell, and several gangsters. The mess attracted the attention of the McClellan Committee (officially the U.S. Senate Select Committee on Improper Activities in the Labor or Management Field), which was on the prowl for labor corruption. Hearings in Portland in 1957, managed by

Paul Bunyan. Kenton's Paul Bunyan was a typical Portland DIY project before anyone knew those initials. Because Oregon's celebration of a century of statehood in 1959 took place at the Portland Expo Center, members of the Kenton Business Club decided to greet visitors driving up North Interstate Avenue with some local color. Volunteer iron workers fabricated and erected an I-beam skeleton, covered it with wire mesh, and troweled on concrete skin and clothing. Half a century later, Paul's stout presence is a reminder of Portland's historic connections to its region, even as Tri-Met nudged him over a few yards to make room for the fourth spoke of our light-rail network. (Photo by author)

the committee Chief Counsel Robert Kennedy, gave the city the very worst kind of publicity.

Meanwhile, the affair rebounded in local politics. Mayor Peterson was running for reelection in 1956 against Terry Schrunk, a labor-backed Democrat and former firefighter who had previously been elected Multnomah County sheriff. Peterson and Purcell accused Schrunk of being on the take and ignoring vice operations. Despite some potentially damning testimony, the grand jury decided that Schrunk's accusers lacked credibility and declined to indict him. Weeks later, Schrunk defeated Peterson by 38,000 votes. He would survive further accusations from Robert Kennedy and the McClellan Committee and win three more terms, serving as mayor through 1972.

It was fear of economic failure as much as national embarrassment that roused Portland from its hibernation. As early as 1953, the *Oregon Journal* had posed the question: "Big league city or sad sack town?" The recession of 1958–59 had a painful impact on real estate development and underscored the weakness of downtown businesses. Retailers in the central core bounded by Burnside, Jefferson, and Twelfth did less business in 1960 than they had immediately after the war. The number of people coming downtown for movies, doctor's appointments, and shopping had dropped by a third. The census of 1960 brought another disappointment when it recorded a small loss of population within the city limits (declining from 373,628 to 372,676). Population for the entire metropolitan area was up only 16 percent for the decade—just half the growth rate of booming Seattle.

With its relatively slow growth overall, no one would have described postwar Portland as an "exploding metropolis" like San Jose or Los Angeles. In the understated Portland style, however, more and more residents chose to load their station wagons and head for a house in the suburbs. Clackamas County added 26,000 residents in the 1950s. Washington County added 31,000. Eastern Multnomah County from the city line to the Sandy River was the most popular destination, with a gain of 50,000. The under-engineered lanes of the Banfield Freeway gave "east county" the area's first limited-access freeway as it crept westward from the town of Fairview to Union Avenue and helped to attract families to new subdivisions in Parkrose, Powellhurst, Rockwood, and Gresham. The first generation of shopping centers along 82nd Avenue and 102nd Avenue served auto-oriented suburbanites and set up a direct challenge to downtown businesses. The total suburban population of Multnomah, Washington, and Clackamas counties surpassed that of the City of Portland in 1962.

Compared to the busy and increasingly congested suburbs of the 21st century, the fringes of the metropolitan area were still sparsely developed. In his memoir, *Shot in the Heart,* writer Mikal Gilmore remembered living along Johnson Creek Boulevard on the line between Multnomah and Clackamas counties and the intersection of wealth and privation. Nearby were dense woods, industrial buildings, and "small cheaply built houses that made up the poor part of a neighboring town called Milwaukie. Beyond that was an area of rolling hills, full of stately, privileged homes—the better half of Milwaukie."

Johnson Creek was also located at the center of David James Duncan's novel about the redemptive power of nature, *The River Why*. It is a watercourse that spans social distances and neighborhoods of multiple ages as it flows through the southeastern part of the metropolitan area. He has described his childhood in the 1950s as "falling in love with every creek and river I saw" as his family moved from place to place in Portland's eastern suburbs.

Growth of the ring of one-story suburbs depended on aid from the federal government. The loan insurance and guarantee programs of the Federal Housing Administration and the Veterans Administration primed a building boom that added more than 300,000 housing units in the metropolitan area by 1980. Federal grants for parks, planning, and especially sewers made it economically feasible to build the new neighborhoods that thousands of Portlanders preferred. Without this aid, growth in Washington and Multnomah counties would have slowed drastically after 1970.

An intangible factor that prodded Portland into action was a change in the population mix. Portland was an aging city at the middle of the 20th century. Despite the influx of young workers during the war years, Portland had far more than its share of retirement-age residents. The median age in the city in 1950 was over 35, compared to 30 for the United States as a whole. By the early sixties, however, a steady decline in the number of elderly voters reduced the power of the group most likely to vote against tax increases. In their place came the most rapidly growing group of Portlanders, men and women in the ambitious years from the late teens to the early thirties, who were likely to see the benefits of an active local government.

The key step in Portland's revitalization was the use of the federal urban renewal program to remake the southern edge of downtown. Portland planners had toyed with urban renewal in the early 1950s but found little support in the unadventurous political climate. In 1956, however, members of the Planning Commission and City Council designated 54 square blocks of the South Portland neighborhood as an urban renewal district. Their intention was to clear the land for a planned coliseum.

East-side Portlanders had complained for decades that city buildings were always located on the wrong side of the Willamette for the majority of citizens. Now the old feud heated up. Urban renewal went forward, but a Veterans Memorial Coliseum on the west side did not, thanks to the pesky voters. Business interests east of the river (the Lloyd Corporation was getting set to build a big east-side shopping mall) put an initiative on the ballot to require any new coliseum to be built on the east side of the Willamette, and in May 1956, Portlanders voted to put a coliseum on the east side by a majority of 303

Shaarie Torah synagogue. Organized in 1905 as the first Orthodox synagogue in the Pacific Northwest, Shaarie Torah synagogue utilized a former Presbyterian Church that it moved to Southwest First and Hall. In the face of the South Auditorium urban renewal project, the congregation decided to move the building to another location, only for it to break apart while being moved on July 3, 1952. It rested in the street for six weeks before being demolished. The congregation built a new synagogue on Southwest Park, only to be displaced by I-405, and moved again to Northwest Lovejoy and Twenty-Fifth in 1965. (Photo by Clyde Putnam Jr., courtesy Thomas Robinson)

out of a total of 128,423 votes cast. Appalled city leaders put the question back on the ballot in November, and the voters stubbornly reaffirmed their choice.

Federal administrators, persuaded by the city's plaintive portrait of South Portland as a hopeless slum in need of clearance, refused to transfer their grant to the east side. There is no doubt that South Portland was simultaneously an eyesore and a real neighborhood. The 84 acres inside the project boundaries were a jumble of junkyards, marginal businesses, low-rent apartments, and abandoned storefronts that had lost much of their usefulness with the disappearance of streetcar and interurban service. Most of the area's buildings were survivors from the 19th century, and 60 percent were officially substandard. Rundown hotels and narrow streets were an eyesore to commuters and housewives heading downtown from the southwest hills. At the same time, many residents remembered the days when South Portland had been the first stop for Italian and Jewish immigrants, with the shops and social organizations that eased the transition to American life. The Development Commission evacuated 2,300 people before the bulldozers arrived. A third were over sixty years old; two-thirds lived alone or as couples without children. Nearly all depended on cheap rents and found companionship in informal neighborhood networks.

The other blow to hit South Portland was what was variously called the Foothills Freeway, or Stadium Freeway. The initial plan was a route that swung close to Civic Stadium as it came south off the planned Fremont Bridge and then made a tight turn eastward between Southwest Clay and Market streets. Motorists who joined from the west would come roaring down the Sunset Freeway and have a straight shot downhill to Fourth Avenue before they'd have to slam on the brakes for a tight right turn onto the Marquam Bridge. One early sketch even showed the freeway tunneling *under* the Civic Auditorium.

This was the alignment that everyone in city government planned for. The Clay-Market alignment was expected to stabilize downtown, defining a compact center by letting autos zip off the freeway directly into the retail and office core. Land in the urban redevelopment district south of Market would be available for surface parking until it was gradually filled with new construction. Portland State College could grow in peaceful isolation from the bustling downtown, perhaps relocating to Southwest First and Lincoln and sharing parking with the proposed Coliseum. But engineers for the Oregon Highway Department had a different idea. Rather than letting the highway run adjacent to Lincoln Hall, St. Mary's Academy, and the Civic Auditorium in a "concrete-walled box canyon," in 1960 they opted to swing it farther south in the interest of creating smoother curves and a lower cost.

Compared to the architecturally bombastic Aztec-style temples and concrete launching pads built in urban renewal areas all over the United States, the plan for South Portland, prepared by the firm of Skidmore, Owings and Merrill, warrants at least a B-plus for handsome urban design. The plan follows the hillside contours with small parks, gardens, and walkways that preserve pedestrian scale. The new office towers and high-rise apartments work with the site rather than overwhelm it. The Lovejoy and Forecourt (Keller) fountains flow, in a seemingly natural pattern, across their sloping site. The successful start of the "South Auditorium" renewal project made it easy for the city council to extend the boundaries of the project north to Market Street in 1966 and to designate another 48-acre renewal zone to assist the expansion of Portland State College.

The east side of the Willamette also witnessed changes that eliminated old neighborhoods. In a warm morning drizzle on August 1, 1960, Mayor Schrunk snipped a 100-foot ribbon to open the Lloyd Center shopping mall.

Downtown in 1948. Southwest Broadway was the heart of Portland nightlife in the 1940s and 1950s, with hotels, clubs, and movie palaces. This photo is from December 1948. The Paramount was repurposed in 1984 as the Arlene Schnitzer Concert Hall of the Portland Center for the Performing Arts. (Photo by Allan deLay, courtesy Thomas Robinson)

Governor Mark Hatfield watched 700 homing pigeons explode from their cages to carry news of the opening to 29 Northwest cities. Lloyd Center was the climax of a dream by California oil millionaire Ralph Lloyd, who had begun to buy up east-side Portland real estate in the 1920s with the vision of building an alternate downtown close to the concentration of population. Despite suspicion from downtown businesses and banks, Lloyd opened a Sears

Lovejoy Columns. Tom Stefopoulos, a Greek immigrant, painted fantastic designs on the columns that supported the Lovejoy Street ramp off the Broadway Bridge while working as a railroad nightwatchman between 1948 and 1952. Years after this photograph was taken, two columns were saved when the city removed the ramp to encourage development of the River District; they have been repositioned along Northwest Tenth between Everett and Flanders. (Photo by Larry Smith, courtesy Thomas Robinson)

store (the building was later converted to the headquarters for Metro) and dug the foundation for a hotel before the Great Depression put his plans on hold. But he continued to acquire land, and he owned nearly a hundred blocks in Northeast Portland at his death in 1953.

Over the next three years the Lloyd Corporation unfolded plans for a massive shopping center only five minutes from the center of Portland. Downtown merchants watched with dismay and tried to agree on ways to ease their parking problems. Their reactions included worry about downtown's decline and anger over the east-side vote on the coliseum. Financing for the shopping mall came not from local banks but from the Prudential Insurance Company.

The Lloyd Corporation broke ground in April 1958, and opened the mall 27 months later. *Business Week* in 1960 noted that Lloyd Center's 1.2 million square feet of rentable space and its eighty-plus stores gave Portland the nation's largest urban shopping center, a distinction that, of course, lasted only a few years. *Time* called it a "consumer's cornucopia" for the 595,000 people who lived within a 20-minute drive.

Between Lloyd Center and the river was the new Memorial Coliseum, which opened in 1960 at the east end of the Broadway Bridge with a performance of "Holiday on Ice." Its construction had leveled the homes of hundreds of African American families. Along with I-5, the Coliseum wiped out the heart of Portland's African American neighborhood. Gone were houses, fraternal lodges, and jazz clubs that had thrived in the 1940s and 1950s. The effects of redevelopment in Lower Albina were a mirror image of the effects on South Portland.

For the better part of a generation, Portland was a city that could not quite make up its mind between investing in the east side or west side, between growth and stagnation. City Commissioner Bill Bowes summed up the problem in 1943 when he remarked, "I hear people say that they long for the day when Portland can return to what it was before our present industrial progress." Bowes for one had no interest in looking backward: "We are standing at the doorway of a new Portland and a great opportunity." Other Portlanders took 15 or 20 years to reach the same conclusion. The *Oregonian* announced the start of a Portland building boom in 1958, but the real importance of Lloyd Center, Memorial Coliseum, and the new apartment towers that replaced South Portland was to show that the sober city on the Willamette was again poised to change—for better or for worse.

Harbor Drive. From the 1910s to the 1960s, Portland rebuilt for the automobile. Transportation officials widened existing streets, upgraded bridges, drove tunnels through the West Hills, and built multilane expressways like Harbor Drive, designed to keep truck traffic off narrow downtown streets. This photograph looks north from Market and Clay. (Portland City Archives, A 2005-001.272)

Chapter 7
The Portland Revolution

Proper Portlanders got a scare when they opened the May 1, 1968, edition of the *Oregon Journal*. "Hippies Might 'Make Scene' in Portland This Summer" was the headline over a story that warned that 20,000 longhairs from San Francisco, already tripped out from 1967's Summer of Love, were planning to head to the Rose City for the summer. An *Oregon Journal* reporter passed the story along to *Newsweek*, whose May 20 item on Portland as "The Hippie's New Nirvana" seemed to validate the fear. The new Haight-Ashbury was supposed to be Lair Hill, another neighborhood where an aging population that made for housing vacancies, low rents, and proximity to downtown had already attracted many of Portland homegrown hippies.

The story was false, the result of a planted rumor, but city officials took it seriously. Lair Hill Park *was* a hippie hangout and a site for countercultural events. The staff at Neighborhood House and the Junior Museum (now the Children's Museum and then located in the park) were not happy when hippies ran children off the softball field or tossed firecrackers at kids. The director of the museum wrote Parks Commissioner Frank Ivancie to complain about the "disgusting talk and exaggerated lovemaking" that drove away families and children. Ivancie had already targeted hippies with a "no wading" rule for Lovejoy Fountain, recently opened to grace the urban renewal area in 1967. Now he acted in July 1968 to impose a curfew at Lair Hill Park. The result was a summer of arrests, court challenges (the curfew law had to be rewritten twice), and local tourism as suburbanites cruised the neighborhood to ogle the longhairs, and maybe to score some weed.

Ivancie's response may have been over the top, but 1968 was a tense and bitter "year of the barricades" across the globe. The Tet Offensive in February had shaken confidence that the United States could win in Vietnam. The assassination of Martin Luther King Jr. on April 4 had ignited riots in cities across the country. Radical students shut down Columbia University in late April. Across the Atlantic, students took to the streets in Italy, Spain, and Berlin. French students fought police in the Paris streets in the first days of May, radical industrial workers called a general strike, and the government nearly toppled before the disturbance subsided. Still to come were the assassination of Robert Kennedy, the police riot at the Democratic Party convention in Chicago, and the Soviet invasion of Czechoslovakia that crushed the democratic reforms and hopes of "Prague Spring."

City Hall officials didn't face Soviet tanks like Alexander Dubček, but they certainly felt like they were surrounded by assaults on the city's comfortable equilibrium. While hippies and their supporters in Lair Hill confronted city officials over lifestyle preferences and free speech, African Americans in Albina were challenging the Portland establishment about basic opportunities for life and livelihoods.

The federal Model Cities program, created in 1966, gave local leaders more than they had bargained for. The program was intended to concentrate federal and local resources on a few selected neighborhoods that would become "models" for revitalization. It also required community participation in setting goals and priorities. The city picked a set of north and northeast neighborhoods with large African American populations and let residents shape the action plan. Delivered in December 1968, the plan was a shocker because it spoke openly about racial discrimination in a city whose white leaders maintained that Portland did not have a race problem. City Commissioners Frank Ivancie and Stanley Earl carefully edited the word "ghetto" out of the document. The Portland Development Commission was furious that the report called out the unequal impact of urban renewal on poor neighborhoods. The Portland School Board was outraged, calling the problem analysis "vicious," "irresponsible," "erroneous," "prejudiced," and "bitter" (this last adjective was certainly true). The city council took four months to accept an amended report, which launched a five-year neighborhood improvement effort that would bolster social services and build community leadership.

The Black Panther Party added radical voices to the advocacy and social service work of the Model Cities staff, the Urban League, and the Albina Ministerial Alliance. Never numbering more than a few dozen, the Panthers preferred direct action to committee meetings. They offered a free breakfast program out of the Highland Park United Church of Christ in 1969, opened the Fred Hampton People's Health Clinic on North Russell Street in the same year, and added a dental clinic in 1970. As in other cities, the Panthers directly challenged the police, with member Kent Ford successfully suing them for assault after his arrest for the nonexistent crime of inciting to riot.

The riot in question had rocked Northeast Portland from June 14 to June 17, 1969. It started when a Friday-night confrontation between police and young African Americans turned ugly. Disturbances lasted through the weekend. At least twenty buildings burst into flames along Union Avenue and adjacent streets like Alberta. Future mayor Tom Potter, then a police officer, remembered the view from the corner of Union and Fremont: "Every building in my line of sight was on fire." The unrest ended without loss of life, but it devastated the Union Avenue business corridor, which had once been lined with businesses started by German immigrants who lived in the nearby Sabin neighborhood.

Disorder moved to the west side in 1970. President Nixon's decision to mount a large-scale U.S. invasion into Cambodia at the end of April triggered student protests that led to the tragic death of four Kent State University students from National Guard bullets on May 4. Student strikes quickly closed more than 400 campuses across the country, including Portland State University. Some of the participants in the PSU strike that began on May 6 erected tents and occupied the South Park Blocks, disrupting traffic and business as

Park Blocks riot. Portland State University exploded into violence on May 11, 1970, when police moved forcibly to remove crowds protesting against the American invasion of Cambodia and the deaths at Kent State University. Students had removed barricades from the Park Blocks but argued that a first aid tent had a valid permit. The Tactical Operations Platoon, recently formed for riot control, thought otherwise, charging into students gathered in front of the tent and scattering them with a cascade of truncheon blows. (Portland City Archives, A 2004-005)

well as the university. After nearly a week, Mayor Schrunk and Commissioner Ivancie decided to quash the strike. When protesters failed to follow orders to take down a properly permitted first aid tent in the Park Blocks, a hundred police in white helmets and riot gear swept across the scene and sent more than two dozen people to hospital treatment.

Four months later came the riot that didn't happen. The American Legion was bringing tens of thousands of members to town for a convention beginning August 30. Angry antiwar activists, who clustered informally under the banner of the People's Army Jamboree, began to talk about disrupting the gathering, floating vague plans that the FBI and state officials took seriously. To blunt the danger, Governor Tom McCall offered the option of bread and circuses—otherwise known as the Vortex I music festival, held at Milo McIver State Park in Clackamas County. A few longhairs suggested the idea to McCall's crew-cut assistant Ed Westerdahl, who sold it to his boss. Well within the Portland metropolitan region, McIver Park was a perfect site, close enough to the city to attract celebrants in the thousands, surrounded by fields for parking, and distant enough to keep people away from the Legionnaires. The result was Woodstock West, without the mud and chaos. Law enforcement officials deliberately ignored pot smoke and nudity among the 35,000 young people and gawkers, who drifted peacefully home at the end of the festival. Meanwhile, a thousand or so protesters had marched and chanted through downtown without incident (aided by President Nixon's decision to cancel a speech to the convention).

In the midst of these violent confrontations and counterculture festivals, other changes were in the air as well, in the form of grassroots activism led by people just a touch older—or perhaps more serious—than the hippies. Over the course of a decade, from the late 1960s to late 1970s, constructive activism by folks we can call quality-of-life liberals fueled a middle-class neighborhood revolution whose effects are still obvious in the progressive Portland of the 21st century.

Perhaps the iconic—and most photogenic—event was a picnic on August 19, 1969. On a summer day when the mountains and coast beckoned many Portlanders, 250 adults and 100 children spread their blankets and opened their coolers and baskets on a barren strip between four lanes of busy traffic on Front Avenue and an even busier four lanes on Harbor Drive, nearly the precise spot where the pioneers had erected Portland's first buildings. The sponsor was an informal group who called themselves Riverfront for People. Organizers Allison and Bob Belcher were there with their kids—aged 18 months and 3 years—carefully leashed so they wouldn't stray into traffic.

Mount Hood Freeway. The so-called Mount Hood Freeway would have connected I-5 to I-205 by cutting through the east side of Portland south of Division Street, as shown in this conceptual drawing. The route was one of several freeway connectors identified in the city's 1966 Comprehensive Plan. Despite the support of the *Oregonian*, Gresham, and Clackamas County, neighborhood opposition and new political leadership from Multnomah County's Don Clark and Portland's Neil Goldschmidt blocked construction and began to turn interest toward rail transit as an alternative to highways. (Author's collection)

Gretchen and Steve Kafoury, neighbors from across the street in the Irvington neighborhood, were there with daughter Deborah (who, 30 years later, would follow in the footsteps of her parents' political careers). The Riverfronters were young and enthusiastic activists who thought that downtown Portland deserved to meet its river across a park rather than an expressway.

The trigger for the picnic was the scheduled demolition of a great beached whale of a building—a two-block edifice built in the 1930s as a public market and later used by the *Oregon Journal*. It sat between Front Avenue and Harbor Drive, which had been opened in 1940 to divert trucks from downtown retail streets. For highway engineers, removing the Journal Building opened up the possibility of *more* lanes for *more* traffic. For the hastily organized Riverfront for People members, it offered the chance to replace concrete with grass, speeding vehicles with people strolling along the downtown riverfront. The City Club of Portland weighed in with a report that called for "varied public use . . . and attractive pedestrian access to the esplanade and the river itself." In October the activists convinced Glenn Jackson, a utility executive who chaired and ruled the powerful state Highway Commission, that a park was at least a possibility. It took two more years of study and debate before completion of the inner freeway loop with the Fremont Bridge gave traffic an alternate route and allowed the city to rip out Harbor Drive. But it was the activists who introduced the idea, fought off halfway measures (burying Harbor Drive in a tube and topping it with sod was one idea), helped put open-minded leaders on the city council, and deserve the credit for what has grown into Tom McCall Waterfront Park.

Riverfront for People was only one part of a much larger grassroots movement. In the half dozen years between 1966 and 1972, largely self-defined community organizations sprang up in every quadrant of the city to fight vigorously for neighborhood conservation in the face of urban renewal and highway construction. On the east side, neighborhood mobilization began in 1967 and 1968 with efforts to provide local input for planning federally assisted programs. Portland Action Committees Together (PACT) organized half a dozen neighborhoods in Southeast Portland to participate in anti-poverty programs. Southeast Uplift was a locally organized equivalent of Model Cities, serving the entire group of southeast neighborhoods that had developed

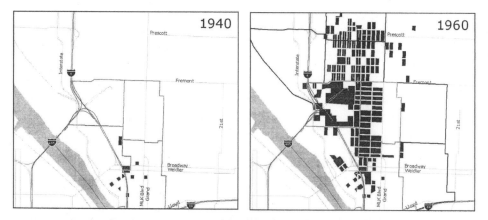

African American Population. Between 1940 and 1960, migration from the South and a discriminatory real estate market combined to form an African American neighborhood in lower Albina. Compiled by the Portland Development Commission from U.S. census data, this map shows blocks at least half of whose residents were non-white. (Institute of Portland Metropolitan Studies, Portland State University)

in the first half of the century, including several low-income communities. On the west side, the Northwest District Association mobilized highly articulate professionals to fight industrial, hospital, and highway expansion. The Corbett-Terwilliger-Lair Hill Park Association came together to resist new urban renewal proposals and respond to plans to convert an old furniture factory into the Johns Landing commercial development. Activists in Lair Hill and Ladd's Addition persuaded the city to designate their neighborhoods as Historic Conservation Districts in 1977, steps that would lead to placement on the National Register of Historic Places. In the mid-1960s, planners had told Mayor Schrunk that Lair Hill was "appropriate for clearance style urban renewal" because it had "few buildings which merit preservation or enhancement." A decade later it had "one of the finest collections of Victorian residential architecture" in the city.

Portlanders organized around issues as well as neighborhoods: women's rights, social and economic justice, grassroots history. *Rain* magazine was an early voice for environmentally sensitive living and community-based responses to global problems. Sunflower Recycling and the Portland Recycling Team both tried to reduce unnecessary consumption while arguing over the best approach. Portlanders could learn about new approaches to old problems through new media like the *Oregon Times* (1971) and *Willamette Week* (1973). KBOO community radio began broadcasting sporadically in 1970, added transmitting power to cover northwest Oregon with a 1,000-watt transmitter, and became independent in 1975, promoting progressive politics and the diversity of local culture.

The list of organizations could go on indefinitely, but scholar-activist Steve Johnson has saved us the trouble with his prize-winning Portland State University PhD dissertation that inventories the transformation of civic life from the 1960s to the 1990s. His findings are striking. In the 1950s and 1960s, Portland was a city of traditional organizations such as fraternal and benevolent societies, ethnic societies, women's clubs, and businessmen's clubs—think Fraternal Order of Eagles, Garden Club, and Kiwanis. Only the City Club and League of Women Voters consistently advocated for public policies. Twenty years later, the roster of organizations was very different: dozens of neighborhood associations and scores of groups advocating for social justice, environmental protection, affordable housing, consumer affairs, and the arts—more than enough to fill an entire *Portland Book: A Guide to Community Resources* in 1979.

It took time for Portland's reputation to catch up with its changing civic life. In 1972, for example, the usually astute political commentator Neal Pierce still thought that "if any West Coast town could be said to have a monopoly on propriety and an anxiousness to 'keep things as they are,' it is Portland, a town of quiet old wealth, discreet culture, and cautious politics." Four years later, in contrast, one of the first systematic comparisons of quality of life among American cities named Portland as the country's "most livable" large city. The strongest contributors to the ranking were indicators of civic involvement like voting turnout, library use, and newspaper readership.

The grassroots ferment fueled a "revolutionary" transition of leadership from an older to a younger generation. Between 1960 and 1970, the proportion of Portlanders aged 15 to 34 had increased from 22 percent to 30 percent. Historian E. Kimbark MacColl found only a 30 percent overlap between lists of the most powerful Portlanders as published in 1969 in the *Labor Press* and the most powerful Oregonians as published in 1975 in the *Oregon Times*. The new generation of voters had more interest in new ideas than in the battles of the past. In response, the average age of Portland City Council members dropped by 15 years between 1969 and 1973. Voters made similar changes in other local governing bodies and in the city's legislative delegation. This generational turnover transformed many basic assumptions of civic debate. The ideas of the older leadership had been formed by the tumultuous years that stretched from the mid-1920s to the mid-1940s. Their goal for the postwar city was social and economic stability. The newer leaders, in contrast, came of age during the optimistic years of the Great Boom of 1945–74, which instilled a sense of possibility rather than limits.

The transition was not always smooth. The 1970 election included a bitter city council battle in 1970 between crusty incumbent Frank Ivancie and young businessman Tom Walsh, who lived in Lair Hill. Ivancie successfully campaigned by branding Walsh as the "king of the hippies." On the positive were the first citywide victories for African American candidates. Charles Jordan, appointed to fill a city council appointment in 1972, won the seat on his own in 1974 and again in 1978. Gladys McCoy was the first African American to win a Multnomah County Commission seat in 1978.

The chief symbol and beneficiary of the political transition was Neil Goldschmidt, elected to the city council in 1970 and as mayor in 1972 at age 32. Goldschmidt served as mayor until 1979, when he became Secretary of Transportation in the Carter administration. Later he served as governor of Oregon, from 1987 to 1990. By the start of his first mayoral term, Goldschmidt and his staff had drawn on a ferment of political and planning ideas and sketched out an integrated strategy for the city that involved the coordination of land use and transportation policies. They were strongly influenced by the 1970

Urban Renewal—Coliseum. Three major projects hit the heavily African American community of Albina in the 1950s and early 1960s—expansion of Interstate Avenue connections to the Steel Bridge, construction of Memorial Coliseum, and the "Minnesota [Avenue] Freeway" or Interstate 5. The Coliseum and its parking lots replaced nearly 500 houses and apartments. This photo shows construction in progress, June 1962. (Photo by Allan deLay, courtesy Thomas Robinson)

census, which showed the effects of a declining proportion of middle-class families on neighborhood diversity and the city tax base. During 1973, 1974, and 1975, Goldschmidt's team brought together a variety of ideas that were waiting for precise definition and articulated them as parts of a single political package that offered benefits for a wide range of citizens and groups.

This so-called "population strategy" emphasized public transportation, neighborhood revitalization, and downtown planning. Improved public transit would improve air quality, enhance the attractiveness of older neighborhoods, and focus activity on downtown. In turn, a vital business center would protect property values in surrounding districts and increase their attractiveness for residential reinvestment. Middle-class families who remained in or moved into inner neighborhoods would patronize downtown businesses, and economic prosperity would support high levels of public services. Neighbor-hood planning would focus on housing rehabilitation and on visible amenities to keep older residential areas competitive with the suburbs.

One essential piece of city strategy was preservation of a user-friendly downtown. Business concerns about suburban competition and parking problems coincided at the end of the 1960s with grassroots efforts like River-front for People. From 1970 to 1972, city leaders merged specific issues into a comprehensive downtown planning process that involved public officials, downtown retailers, property owners, neighborhood groups, and profession-al and civic organizations. The resulting Downtown Plan offered integrated solutions to a long list of problems that Portlanders had approached piece-meal for two generations. It was technically sound because its proposals were based on improvements to access and transportation. It was politically viable because it prescribed trade-offs among different interests as part of a coherent strategy. Specific proposals ranged from a waterfront park and pedestrian-oriented design to high-density retail and office corridors intersecting in the center of downtown. The Citizens Advisory Committee made variety, activity, and people the interlocking foundations of the plan. The goal was to design downtown to be everybody's neighborhood—a district that would offer something for workers, shoppers, pedestrians, bus riders, the young, the elderly, commuters, and permanent residents.

The direct complement to revitalizing downtown was to recycle older neighborhoods built from the 1880s through the 1930s. The city used Hous-ing and Community Development funds and leveraged private capital with tax-free borrowing for an extensive housing rehabilitation program that met demands from newly active neighborhood groups. Inflation of suburban housing costs in the 1970s also helped to retain families in older, affordable neighborhoods. Several neighborhoods between downtown and the base of the West Hills experienced gradual gentrification from new residents look-ing for Portland's closest version of a sophisticated urban environment. The bungalow belt on the east side of the Willamette attracted a new generation of Portlanders looking for traditional city neighborhoods of 50-by-100-foot lots, trees, sidewalks, and stores within walking distance.

Direct investment policy was accompanied by a political bargain with neighborhood interests. After a series of confrontations between neighbor-hoods and City Hall in the late 1960s, the Goldschmidt administration decided to legitimize and partially co-opt neighborhood activists by incorporating independent neighborhood associations as secondary participants in public de-cisions. The means was the Office of Neighborhood Associations, established in 1974 to help neighborhoods articulate their needs and concerns. Formal acceptance and limited financial support of voluntary neighborhood groups offered a *partial* alternative both to confrontational tactics from grassroots activism and to top-down management of citizen participation from City Hall.

A key connector for the downtown-neighborhood strategy was to shift investment from highways to public transit. As was happening across the country, federal funds allowed a new Tri-County Metropolitan Transit District (TriMet) to buy out the bankrupt Rose City Transit Company in 1969. One of the key features of the Downtown Plan of 1972 was a transit mall (completed in 1978) that increased the speed of bus service, facilitated transfers, and served as a model for similar plans in cities from Denver to Ottawa. The second major transit decision was the 1975 cancellation of the so-called Mount Hood Freeway, a five-mile connector that would have devastated half a dozen lower-middle-class neighborhoods in Southeast Portland. As with Harbor Drive, community protest provided the impetus and political support that allowed Goldschmidt and Multnomah County Commissioner Don Clark to say no to a freeway. Most of the federal money was transferred to build a controversial 15-mile light-rail line from downtown to Gresham as the first leg of the Metropolitan Area Express (MAX) system.

Regional planning takes place within the context of Oregon's 20-year-old statewide land-use planning system. By the end of the 1960s, Willamette Valley residents from Portland to Eugene had begun to view low-density suburbanization as a serious environmental problem that wasted irreplaceable scenery, farmland, and energy. A key document was landscape planner Lawrence Halprin's 1972 report called *The Willamette Valley: Choices for the Future*, which laid out a future of landscape sprawl and clutter in the absence of planning intervention. In the back of Oregonians' minds was a fear of Los Angeles-like suburban sprawl. Second-home subdivisions were explicitly associated with the painful example of California and roundly condemned by Governor Tom McCall in 1972.

> There is a shameless threat to our environment and to the whole quality of life—the unfettered despoiling of the land. Sagebrush subdivisions, coastal condomania, and the ravenous rampage of suburbia in the Willamette Valley all threaten to mock Oregon's status as the environmental model for the nation. . . . The interests of Oregon for today and for the future must be protected from grasping wastrels of the land.

Legislation in 1973 created what was in essence a farmland protection program and required local jurisdictions to prepare comprehensive plans in harmony with statewide planning goals. From the very start, however, the program evolved from a purely reactive effort to fend off erosion of the state's farm economy to a positive attempt to shape a particular urban form. One key element was the requirement that every municipality or metropolitan area establish an urban growth boundary, adopted by the Portland area in 1979. Required by law to embrace a 20-year supply of developable land, the urban growth boundary is intended to prevent sprawl by providing for "an orderly and efficient transition from rural to urban use." Within the boundary, the burden of proof rests on opponents of land development. Outside the boundary, the burden rests on developers to show that their land is easily supplied with necessary services and not worth retention as open space or farmland.

The state planning system has been coupled with the nation's only directly elected regional government. Voters created a multifunctional regional

Lovejoy Fountain. Landscape architect Lawrence Halprin designed the Lovejoy and Forecourt (now Keller) fountains as elements in a flowing "sequence of open spaces" through the South Auditorium urban renewal project that were "choreographed for movement with nodes for quiet and contemplation, action and inaction, hard and soft." His wife Anna Halprin, a well-known dancer, enhanced the effect with literal choreography, following the suggestion that the Lovejoy plaza should have "dance events with dancers all over." In 1971, the Lovejoy Fountain was not yet surrounded by tall buildings and partially isolated from the rest of the city. (Portland City Archives, A 2005-005)

government—Metro—in 1978 and expanded its independence and purview by approving a home rule charter in 1992. Not every voter who cast her ballot in favor of strong regional government may have known what she was doing, but the fact remains that Portland is one of the few metropolitan areas that has voluntarily established and enhanced such a metropolitan level government that handles regional land use and transportation planning, regional parks, and regional facilities like the convention center and zoo.

Metro's regional services are a reminder of the importance of thinking at the scale of the metropolitan area. Americans tend to assume that livable cities are small cities, and many Portlanders long enjoyed being told that they lived in an overgrown town. In fact, a city is truly livable only if it is big enough. To give all its residents the opportunity to realize and utilize their abilities, a city needs an adequate base of public and private resources. Residents benefit from the opportunity to interact with others of different backgrounds and cultures. A fully livable city needs the population and wealth to support higher education and the arts. It also needs to be large enough to offer a variety of jobs and to develop the sophisticated business services that promote economic innovation and spin-off industries.

The threshold population for a truly livable metropolitan area is a million plus, a threshold that Portland passed in late 1969. The four counties of the federally defined metropolitan area (Multnomah, Clackamas, Washington, Clark) had 822,000 residents in 1960; 1,007,000 in 1970; and 1,240,000 in 1980. Although the City of Portland was where the new politics was happening, outlying communities were where the majority of new people were settling. Taken together, suburban Washington, Clackamas, and eastern Multnomah counties surpassed the city of Portland in total population in the mid-1950s and in retail sales in 1972. The number of jobs located in the suburbs matched the number inside the central city by the early 1980s.

At the same time, key communities grew from small towns to substantial cities. Gresham grew from only 10,000 people in 1970 to 68,000 in 1990 and to 102,000 in 2010. In those same years, Hillsboro grew from 15,000 to 38,000 and then to 91,000; the numbers for Beaverton are 18,000 to 53,000 to 87,000. They are the now fourth, fifth, and sixth largest municipalities in Oregon. Across the wide Columbia, annexation helped Vancouver grow from 42,000 in 1970 and 46,000 in 1990 to 166,000 in 2010.

Unlike many metropolitan areas, key suburban municipalities in the Portland regional recognize that they share common interests with the central city. Careful political deal-making has helped to convince the suburban counties and the three largest of the outlying cities—Gresham, Beaverton, and Hillsboro—to accept a staged expansion of the light-rail system, with several arms converging in downtown Portland; this will relieve congestion on key suburban highways. With the exception of Washington County manufacturers, who prefer cross-suburb road improvements, Portland's civic leadership now considers strong public transit to be one of the axioms of regional development—in effect, the second "deal" that has structured growth politics for more than three decades.

The expansion of electronics industries was a vital part of the suburban transformation. Companies like Tektronix and Electro-Scientific Instruments (ESI) had originated in empty storefronts and warehouses in Southeast Portland in the early 1950s. As business grew, Tek, ESI, and other electronics companies built new facilities on vacant land in Washington County and Clackamas County, as did the California electronics giant Intel, which built its first Oregon plant in Aloha in 1976. Spin-off companies like Floating Point Systems, from Tektronix, and Lattice Semiconductor, from Intel, and local plants of other national and international electronics firms added to the mix, so that the area's "Silicon Forest" on the west side of the Willamette in the early 1980s employed an estimated 25,000 assembly line workers, electronic engineers, and software writers. High-tech jobs accounted for 10 percent of all of Oregon's nonagricultural job growth from 1975 to 1982, ranking the state sixth among all fifty states in terms of relative growth of the high-tech sector.

A second key to the boom of the later 1960s and 1970s was the revitalization of Portland's role as a river city. The port lost business to Seattle in the 1960s when the Docks Commission failed to modernize shipping facilities and ignored the growing market for containerized cargo. Under the persistent prodding of Governor Tom McCall, city leaders agreed to merge the Docks Commission into the Port of Portland in 1970 as an economic development measure. In 1973, the legislature expanded the port to serve Washington and Clackamas counties as well as Multnomah. These decisions helped Portland regain ground lost to its West Coast rivals of Seattle, Tacoma, and Oakland. Japanese imports such as Hondas and Toyotas made—and still make—Portland the largest auto port on the West Coast. Although Terminal 6 has been developed as a major container dock, the port struggled to maintain multiple-carrier container services as the global shipping industry consolidated.

In any event, Portland benefited from the growing importance of American trade with the Pacific Rim. In 1970, U.S. commerce with foreign nations out of West Coast ports accounted for 17 percent of the national total; by 1983 it accounted for 24 percent. Every month ships left Portland for Melbourne and Singapore, Kobe and Yokohama, Penang and Pusan, Hong Kong and

Charles Jordan. Charles Jordan was the first African American elected to a citywide political office. Appointed to city council to fill a vacancy in 1974, he won reelection for two additional terms and later served as director of the Portland Parks Bureau after leaving electoral politics. (Portland City Archives, A 2005-005)

Taiwan, Callao, Valparaiso, and Panama. They arrived in Portland carrying steel, petroleum, palm oil, autos, and general merchandise. They departed with wheat, lumber, wood chips, and even frozen French fries for McDonald's restaurants in Tokyo. The real value of Portland trade in constant dollars tripled between 1966 and 1983.

The political ferment of the 1970s continued to bubble into the 1980s, but the economy did not. The United States experienced a sharp economic recession in 1981–82. Much of the national economy recovered by mid-decade, but Oregon and Portland remained trapped in the downturn for several more years, particularly because of their dependence on a now crippled wood products industry, which devastated many rural communities and reduced their ability to draw on goods and services from the metropolis. As had been true before, a hiccup in the California real estate market meant a bellyache for Oregon. From 1981 to 1985, the Portland metropolitan area found itself in the same situation as Rust Belt cities like Youngstown and Newark, actually losing more residents than it gained through immigration, as people looked for opportunities elsewhere.

Nevertheless, signs of progress were easy to spot in the heart of the city. The multicolored Portland Building designed by Michael Graves opened in

1982, giving Portland a tourist-worthy architectural attraction, if not a building where anyone actually wanted to work. In 1984, Pioneer Courthouse
Square replaced a two-level parking ramp with a space intended to be Portland's "living room." The McCormick Pier apartments in 1982 and River-
Place condominiums in 1985 responded to the middle class's new interest in
downtown living. The Performing Arts Center that opened both new and
refurbished performance spaces in 1984–85 was another addition to the heart
of downtown, which some eastsiders could soon reach on the MAX line that
carried its first passengers from Gresham in 1986.

Left unanswered in the mid-1980s was whether these new landmarks
were an end or a new beginning. Was Portland winding up its agenda from
the creative seventies and preparing to settle back into its earlier ways as a
risk-averse community? Or was it ready to extend its innovative trajectory as
business recovered and resources came available? Was it destined to be another
comfortable, unexciting river town like Cincinnati, or would change continue?
Would clean, earnest Portland grow into a cooler version of Seattle without the
brand-name fixation . . . become as hip as Austin, but with conifers . . . look
like Vancouver (B.C.) with a south-of-the-border accent? As the ultimate test,
would it have enough action to keep transplanted New Yorkers awake?

Artists

Portland in the generation after World War II was a long way from national centers of art and culture. Its art museum had scored a coup in 1913 as the only venue outside New York to display selections from the famous Armory Show that had introduced Americans to modern art, but its permanent collections were thin. The city had no literary outlets with New York connections, no coteries of competitive collectors, no throngs of newly minted millionaires looking to make a big splash with flashy donations. Portland was not a San Francisco or Paris that attracted ambitious newcomers who wanted to make their cultural mark on a big stage.

Nevertheless, during the years of social and political transformation after the mid-20th century, Portland developed a vibrant local arts scene, often with individuals who arrived for mundane reasons like jobs and family and stayed to become mainstays of local culture.

The preferred style of Portland's midcentury artists resonated with the city's emerging grassroots political culture. Key figures earned national and international reputations, but they spread their influence locally as teachers and mentors. Writers and visual artists remained rooted and connected to the city and region—provincials in the most positive sense of creative individuals deeply engaged with their community, city, and region.

Poet William Stafford (1914–93) exemplifies the Portland style. He grew up in Kansas, served as a conscientious objector during World War II (the subject of his first book), and accepted an offer to teach at Lewis and Clark College in 1948. He spent some years in the mid-1950s earning a PhD from the University of Iowa and filling one-year jobs at other colleges, but he returned permanently to Portland in 1957. The first of his dozens of books of poetry appeared in 1960. *Traveling Through the Dark*, his second book, won the National Book Award in 1963. The ambiance of northwestern Oregon suffused his work, whether in a quiet meditation like "Camping at Lost Lake" or his masterly commentary on worldly ambition in "My Party the Rain."

Ursula Le Guin (b. 1929) spent the first three decades of her life in places far more sophisticated than Portland (Berkeley, Boston, New York, Paris), and came to the Northwest in 1958 only because her husband, Charles, took a position in the History Department at Portland State College. Her base of operations was a basement desk in their Willamette Heights house, shaded by tall trees, shadowed by Forest Park, and misted by northwestern clouds. She made her first sales in 1962 and published her breakthrough novel, *The Left Hand of Darkness*, in 1969, followed in the 1970s by *The Lathe of Heaven*,

The Dispossessed, and the first of the Earthsea books. Her work spans genres — science fiction, magical realism, fantasy, historical fiction, poetry, criticism. In the 1970s and 1980s she was an active workshop teacher and mentor to other fine local writers like Molly Gloss. *The Lathe of Heaven* is her only novel set explicitly (and fantastically) in Portland, but the regional landscape pervades her work—the Oregon high desert in *The Tombs of Atuan*, the damp Oregon coast in *Searoad*, and the islands and fjords of the Salish Sea in some of the Earthsea tales.

Portland may have been an even greater stretch for Michele (Mike) Russo. Raised in Italy and New England, Russo (1909–2004) arrived in Portland with a BFA from Yale and a job at the school of Portland Museum Art School (now the Pacific Northwest College of Art). He taught there until 1974 and co-founded the Portland Center for the Visual Arts in 1973. Along with colleagues like Mel Katz and Manuel Izquierdo, he introduced generations of students and other Portlanders to contemporary trends in the visual arts. In a 1983 interview available from the Smithsonian Institute Archives of American Art, Russo commented on his adopted home: "I love this region . . . I think I have a kind of idealism which I see in the region . . . I see it in the environment, and I see it in the people. And so I feel a very strong regional identification."

Russo, Le Guin, and Stafford marked a transition. They were neither gifted dilettantes like C. E. S. Wood nor local-color specialists like writer Stewart Holbrook (1893–1964). Instead, they worked for national and international audiences without losing their connection to Portland, and they paved the way for younger artists. Filmmaker Gus Van Sant, who had a tenuous connection to Portland from his last year of high school, returned in the 1980s to make a trio of movies about the gritty side of Portland (*Mala Noche* in 1985, *Drugstore Cowboy* in 1989, and *My Own Private Idaho* in 1990). Musician Thomas Lauderdale, Grant High School graduate and toast of France with his group, Pink Martini, is firmly based in Portland. The dynamite women rockers of Sleater-Kinney chose to live in Portland over both Olympia and Seattle at the start of the 21st century. They put the band aside in 2006, but the members were still living in town in 2011, making music and writing television shows. And there are hundreds of other women and men in their twenties and thirties who moved to Portland as artists and artisans to make plays and poetry, music and murals.

Chapter 8
Portland Looks Forward

Portlanders enthusiastically adopted two civic icons in the mid-1980s.

In 1985, the city installed *Portlandia* in her niche over the entrance to the newly completed Portland Building. This huge copper statue of a kneeling woman clutching a trident in one hand and reaching out to pedestrians on the Fifth Avenue Transit Mall with the other was based on the figure of "Lady Commerce" on the city seal. On the drizzly autumn morning of October 6, the completed statue was transported by barge up the Willamette from its assembly point in the Northwest Industrial District like a reddish-orange Cleopatra. Thousands of Portlanders turned out in a spontaneous civic celebration. They lined the waterfront, joined Mayor Bud Clark in their canoes and boats, or crowded downtown to see it hoisted into place. Parents lifted their children to touch the outstretched finger as they passed it in the street.

Although reviews of Michael Graves's Portland Building were decidedly mixed, sculptor Raymond Kaskey's creation inspires nearly universal affection. It weighs 6.5 tons and stretches nearly 35 feet high (if Portlandia got to stand up, she would stand 50 feet tall). Kaskey spent three years hammering copper sheeting the thickness of a dime around complex steel frames. The result is the largest work of its kind with the exception of that other copper goddess, New York's Statue of Liberty.

A year later, Portland turned to a very different but complementary symbol in designating the great blue heron as the city's official bird. Mayor Bud Clark, who enjoyed canoeing on the Willamette before the start of a day in City Hall, made frequent references to herons in a welcoming speech to a convention of wildlife managers. Mike Houck, of the Portland Audubon Society, picked up on Clark's interest and suggested giving the bird official status. Everyone on the city council was enthusiastic, and the formal proclamation came in December 1986.

Portlandia in Motion. Portlanders staged an impromptu celebration on October 6, 1985, when the 34-foot-10-inch statue of *Portlandia* was barged from its assembly point in the industrial district to be hauled into place on the Portland Building. (Photo by Hugh Ackroyd, courtesy Thomas Robinson)

If *Portlandia* represents the strength of the city center and civic involve-ment, the blue heron reflects the deep affection that Portlanders hold for their natural surroundings. A bird of rivers and marshes, the blue heron connects contemporary Portland to its origins as a straggling riverfront settlement. It also speaks to the city's ongoing commitment to building a thriving metro-politan region without destroying its natural setting.

By the mid-1990s, urban experts in other parts of the United States thought that Portlanders were carrying through on their commitment. Indeed, the city's press clippings could sometimes be so glowing that residents might wonder if they could measure up to their reputation. To many observers, Portland has been one of the few large metropolitan areas "where it works," to quote a 1990 headline in the *Economist.* An informal poll of planning ex-perts in 1988 rated Portland's efforts to deal with urban design issues among the best in the United States.

Overall, many experts believe that the Portland area is among the nation's most successful in balancing economic growth and environmental protection. Inspection junkets have become a steady contributor to the Portland tourist economy as journalists try to discover "how Portland does it" and civic leaders make the rounds in search of lessons for their own city—prompting Portland

State University's Institute for Metropolitan Studies to create a First Stop Portland program just to manage requests from visiting delegations. The most common question is how a city can prosper without destroying its natural setting through sprawl. The most frequent answer, as summarized in a federal government report on "America's New Economy and the Challenge of the Cities" (1996), is that metropolitan Portland prospers *because* it is compact and efficient. As HUD Secretary Henry Cisneros noted, "Communities that emphasize cooperation over competition within their region have succeeded in expanding economic prosperity and creating jobs in the New Economy."

In the contemporary media world, "best city" lists have proliferated in magazines and on websites—to the delight of local boosters. Over the past twenty years, Portland has frequently appeared near the top of urban livability rankings aimed at groups as disparate as working women and bicycling enthusiasts. Some of the rankings are rather specialized, although it is nice to know that experts think that Portland is the most polite U.S. city, the skateboarding capital of the nation, the seventh leanest city (perhaps because of all the skateboarders), and the best city in which to have a baby. Reports also tell us that tourists give it high marks as clean, green, and safe but low marks for luxury shopping. The Corporation for National and Community Service has compiled data showing Portland placing second or third in the percentage of residents who volunteered their time during 2002–09, with an average of 48 hours per resident in the latter year (Salt Lake City topped the list and Portland traded places back and forth in the rankings with the Twin Cities). And an international consulting firm that ranks cities worldwide to help companies decide about international locations and assignments put Portland at 45th in 2010, tied with Chicago and Lisbon, just behind Barcelona and just ahead of Madrid.

So what happened in the turn-of-the-21st-century decades to put Portland in such fast company?

The city certainly got bigger. The four-county metropolitan area had 1,334,000 people in 1980 and 2,236,000 in 2010. Most of the growth occurred in the core counties, but the Census Bureau also stretched the county boundaries as employment patterns linked previously rural areas to the urban or suburban economy. The census experts added Yamhill County in 1990, Columbia County in 2000, and Skamania County, Washington, in 2010. The changes didn't mean that everyone in Stevenson or McMinnville worked in downtown Portland, but it did recognize those commuting on Washington Highway 14 into Clark County or Oregon Highway 99 into Washington County. The growth kept the Portland metro area just out of the top twenty metropolitan areas in population. At 23rd in 2010, it was a little smaller than Denver and Pittsburgh but larger than Sacramento and Cincinnati.

The City of Portland also grew within expanding territory. Population within the city limits had been stable from 1950 (at 374,000) to 1970 (at 382,000) and then dipped to 365,000 in 1980, beginning to follow the pattern of many other American cities where central neighborhoods emptied out. Aggressive annexation in the 1980s and 1990s reversed the trend, adding most of the territory between I-205 and Southeast 162nd, while Gresham's boundary grew westward at the same time to meet Portland. In 2000, Portland had grown to 529,000 people, and it grew to 583,000 in 2010 as a result of new infill housing and growing immigrant families.

Growth of the city and metropolitan area has also changed Portland into a much more cosmopolitan community than it was a generation earlier. In 1980 the largest racial minority in the three-county core was 32,000 African Americans who constituted 3 percent of the population, followed by Asian Americans at 2 percent. Latinos and Hispanics, who can be of any race, also made up 2 percent of the tri-county total. After three decades in which the United States—and Portland—benefited from very substantial immigration, the Latino/Hispanic population had burgeoned to 192,000, or 13 percent of the Multnomah-Washington-Clackamas county total. The proportion of people identifying solely as Asians or Pacific Islanders had quadrupled to 8 percent with a count of 114,000. Native American/Indian and African American numbers had also grown, but at roughly the same rate as the counties as a whole, with shares of, respectively, 1 percent and 4 percent.

Throughout all of these changes, the metropolitan area has remained strongest at its center, as is neatly exemplified by the baseball dilemma of recent years. The problem for promoters and city officials has been where to locate a new baseball stadium. Failure to resolve it stymied efforts to attract a Major League Baseball team when the Montreal Expos were looking for a new home (they eventually became the Washington Nationals). It also drove Portland's Triple-A baseball team out of town in 2010 when PGE Park (Multnomah Stadium or Civic Stadium to those with good memories) was re-allocated to Major League Soccer and no one could find a place for even a small replacement stadium.

The crucial issue was the lack of empty or derelict land. Cities like Cleveland, Denver, Baltimore, and Pittsburgh have used new baseball parks to occupy underutilized acres of old industrial and warehouse land on the fringe of their downtowns, hoping with some success for spillover effects on nearby real estate. Portland, in contrast, lacks the "gray area" or "dead zone"

Japanese-American Historical Plaza. The Japanese-American Historical Plaza realized a dream of Portland businessman and civic leader Bill Naito. It sits in Tom McCall Waterfront Park between a heavily used riverside walkway and Naito Parkway (formerly Front Avenue). Designed by Robert Murase, this visually compelling landscape commemorates the internment of Japanese Americans during World War II. (Murase Associates)

of derelict industrial districts and abandoned neighborhoods that typically surround the high-rise core of many cities. There has simply been no place to put a downtown stadium without replacing or displacing active, viable uses.

Plant one point of a giant compass in Pioneer Courthouse Square and draw a circle with a two-mile radius. Inside will be nearly all of the important regional institutions and civic facilities—museums and zoo; sports venues; major performance spaces; convention center; federal, state, and regional government offices; Portland State University; Oregon Health and Science University. The near east side was increasingly recognized as part of the city core with construction of the Oregon Convention Center in 1990, the Oregon Museum of Science and Industry in 1992, and the Rose Garden Arena in 1995 (the latter built largely by software billionaire Paul Allen, owner of the Trail Blazers). The downtown office market was healthier than the suburban market throughout the first decade of the new century, including the real estate collapse of 2008–10. In the third quarter of 2010, the vacancy rate for high-end (class A) office space was 9 percent for the central business district and 23 percent for the suburbs. Apartment and condo towers brought thousands of affluent residents to the Pearl District north of Burnside, to the

River District—the area that used to be the Northern Pacific rail yards—to the blocks west of Broadway, and, slowly, to the South Waterfront.

In the 1980s, Seattle writer Ivan Doig posed a question to readers of the *New York Times:* "Portland is a great place to live, but would you want to visit there?" A quarter century later, the answer was yes. Visitors could stay in a raft of upscale and boutique hotels (newly built or upscaled), eat at restaurants with rave reviews in the New York media, and marvel at Powell's Bookstore. They could comment repeatedly on the city's "European" feel (generally thought to be a good thing) and ride the $50 million aerial tram between OHSU and the South Waterfront, a project intended for practical transportation but increasingly a spot on the tourist itinerary.

Rising above the city center and behind OHSU is a curiosity of urban geography that makes Portland unique among similar-size communities. The set of neighborhoods called the "West Hills" became Portland's upscale residential district with the advent of family automobiles in the 1910s and 1920s. For three generations, the affluent highlanders of King's Heights, Arlington Heights, Willamette Heights, Portland Heights, and Council Crest have enjoyed views of Mount Hood and 10-minute commutes to downtown offices. Protected by elevation from the lower-income residents and mixed uses of the downtown fringe, successful businessmen, ambitious professionals, and heirs of moneyed families have been able to maintain social status and leafy living without needing to leave the city for a refuge in suburbia. They have also found that downtown remains the most convenient place to work and shop.

The social status of living in the West Hills was never in doubt, but that was not the case with many of the streetcar-era neighborhoods on the east side, as evidenced by the richness of community activism in the 1970s and 1980s. The metro-wide inflation of housing values in the mid-1990s, however, confirmed the neighborhoods' attractions for the managerial-professional middle class. Close-in neighborhoods like Irvington-Grant Park-Alameda, Laurelhurst, and Sellwood-Westmoreland felt the effects of this in the 1990s. The wave of reinvestment pushed farther outward in the new century to Woodstock, Montavilla, Rose City Park, University Park, and St. Johns.

The results were obvious to anyone who drove the old streetcar routes, where the vitality of old shopping strips is one of the best indicators that Portland is different from other cities. Portland consumers became familiar with fashionable Northwest Twenty-Third Avenue, friendly Sellwood, and trendy Hawthorne in the 1990s. The new century brought artsy Alberta, super-hip North Mississippi Avenue, and other rivals. Just as important are everyday shopping districts, from Hillsdale in Southwest Portland to Hollywood in

Aerial tram. The 3,300-foot route of the aerial tram connects Oregon Health and Sciences University with the South Waterfront and the Portland Streetcar into downtown. Controversial because costs substantially exceeded initial estimates, it provides a great three-minute ride with superb views of the city. Opened in 2006, it carries more than 1 million one-way passenger trips per year. (Wikimedia Commons)

Northeast Portland and St. Johns in North Portland. Family movie theaters survive in every quadrant, still holding their own against multiplex competition (sometimes with the help of pizza and beer).

The political beneficiaries of the Portland makeover were mayors Bud Clark (1985–92) and Vera Katz (1993–2004). When tavern-owner and neighborhood activist J. E. "Bud" Clark decided to challenge incumbent mayor Frank Ivancie in the May 1984 primary, few experts gave him a chance to win. Clark's last elective office, after all, had been senior class treasurer at Lincoln High School in the late 1940s. In fact, years of activity in Portland neighborhood associations and community service programs had given Clark both name recognition and access to a network of volunteer political workers. While Ivancie misjudged his own campaign strategy and failed to shake his image as an ally of the downtown business establishment, Clark made quiet gains to emerge with a stunning victory—he carried 235 out of 291 precincts. Clark's combination of fiscal conservatism and political populism appealed both to an older generation of neighborhood businesspeople and the new generation of neighborhood activists. A large, friendly man who usually wore a Portland rose in his lapel, Clark made citizens feel at home in City Hall while he carefully scrutinized city budgets and helped get the Convention Center built.

Vera Katz, previously Speaker of the Oregon House of Representatives, followed Bud Clark. A shrewd and strong-minded leader, she was one of the generation of Portlanders drawn into politics during the ferment of the 1970s. Her administration extended many of Clark's initiatives, including community policing. The rate of reported crime fell. The city and Multnomah County worked together to disperse services and shelters for homeless people and those in need of transitional housing. The city also gave renewed attention to promoting new housing at all income levels. The rapid rise of housing prices in the mid-1990s, including the middle-class "discovery" of many old working-class neighborhoods east of the Willamette, made the affordable housing initiative especially urgent.

Indeed, the popularity of inner neighborhoods—undoubtedly a Portland success story—had the side effect of pushing lower-income households toward the suburban ring. In 1980, Killingsworth Street marked the northern edge of African American Portland. Thirty years later, the African American population had shifted northwest along Lombard and northeast toward Parkrose. The number of children living in poverty grew in Clark County, in Washington County, and especially in Multnomah County east of I-205. The largest decreases in poverty were inside the borders of the city of Portland, in the gentrifying neighborhoods that were so attractive to hip tourists and young college graduates.

Portland's increasing ethnic and racial diversity did not spread evenly over the metropolitan area. School enrollment is a sensitive indicator of ethnic patterns—not only for the present but also for years to come. In the 2009–10 school year, 44 percent of the students in Portland Public Schools were members of a federally defined minority group—African American, Asian American, American Indian, or Hispanic. Ethnic variety was greater, not less, in two wide bands outside the city. To the east, the Parkrose school district was the most diverse: 61 percent of its students were members of ethnic minorities. Reynolds followed with 54 percent, then David Douglas with 51 percent and Centennial with 44 percent. A dozen miles to the west was another diverse region: 50 percent of Forest Grove students, 45 percent of Hillsboro students, and 44 percent of Beaverton students were members of minority groups.

In contrast, the area's low minority/high majority band ran across northern Clackamas County, including Oregon City, West Linn-Wilsonville and Lake Oswego. The small Riverdale district, serving the high-toned enclave of Dunthorpe, is the heart of whiteness, at 92 percent. With Asian Americans as its second-largest group, Riverdale looks more like the Fossil and Spray districts in central Oregon than like any other metro school district.

Contained within the aggregated school data were distinct ethnic and immigrant clusters. At the start of the 21st century, Vietnamese residents were most likely to live in east-side neighborhoods three to six miles from downtown Portland. Russians, Ukrainians, and other immigrants from Eastern Europe also lived in these areas; they also favored Clark County. Koreans had established a substantial presence in Beaverton. Hispanics were found both in aging suburban areas with affordable housing and in outlying places like Hillsboro, Forest Grove, and Canby, reflecting their historic role as workers in labor-intensive agriculture. Novelist and essayist Matthew Stadler has described the new suburban reality, in which "the multitude that makes up the life and future of the city" now lives toward its edges rather than its center:

> At the Beaverton Transit Center, Spanish is the common language and buses leave every few minutes for the polyglot strips of Beaverton . . . Manila imports, Korean bulgoki, Dutch oliebollen, taco trucks, nail salons, phone cards, instant credit, barbecue, and prayer candles in a dozen languages rise like a slow tide to fill these endless, outdated strip malls. . . . The stores are odd, their survival miraculous . . . Equipped only with the categories of the 20th-century city, one is barely able to engage this plentitude.

Increasingly cosmopolitan suburbs attracted increasingly sophisticated leaders. An example among many was Gussie McRobert, mayor of Gresham from 1988 to 1998, who advocated for a strong downtown and for economic development. "Gresham was not on the map until Gussie became mayor," according to city council member David Widmark. Thanks to her earlier career in public broadcasting, she also had the skills to talk the acerbic and self-confident critic James Howard Kunstler to a standstill on a tour of the city. Other suburban mayors who pursued annexation, expansion of services, and economic development included Rob Drake in Beaverton (1993–2008) and Tom Hughes in Hillsboro (2001–09).

Portland's regional growth since the mid-1990s has taken place within a consciously adopted planning framework. Metro, as the regional government with responsibility for regional planning, has been the lead agency in responding to expected population growth through its "Region 2040" plan for accommodating up to a million more residents in the four core counties. The 2040 process was remarkable for the breadth of participation, including homebuilders and commercial real estate interests as well as growth management advocates. It was also remarkable for actually changing ideas, starting

Downtown Hillsboro. Located at the terminus of the Westside light-rail line, Hillsboro has been transformed in a half century from the country seat of an agricultural county to a center for high-tech industry. Regional plans identify it as one of the "regional centers" that will help to focus development inside the Urban Growth Boundary. (Wikimedia commons)

as an effort to figure out how far the Portland area should grow and ending with a debate over how best to limit outward expansion. The Metro Council adopted the "Region 2040 Growth Concept" in December 1994 and more detailed measures to implement the plan in late 1996. The plan's broad goals for the next half century are to focus new jobs and housing on downtown Portland, urban and suburban centers, and transportation corridors.

With the east-side MAX light-rail line considered a success, voters approved an 18-mile west-side line to Hillsboro at the start of the 1990s. Portlanders watched with fascination as Tri-Met punched a long tunnel through the West Hills with a 260-foot elevator to serve the Portland Zoo stop (the third-deepest underground rail station in the world) and opened the line in 1998. A third stage in the area's light-rail system ran into trouble, however. Plans called for a long north-south line from Vancouver, Washington, through downtown Portland to Clackamas County. Tri-county voters approved a local contribution in 1994, but Clark County said no to the segment north of the Columbia River in 1995. Then, in November 1995, voters statewide rejected a state contribution to the north-south line. Transit advocates went back to the drawing board to use a combination of local urban renewal money and federal grants for an east-side airport spur (2001), a six-mile line up North Interstate

Avenue (2004), an east-side extension into Clackamas County (2009), and a second Clackamas County line to Milwaukie (expected 2015).

To skeptics, Portland seemed rail crazy. A downtown streetcar (in effect, ultra-light rail) opened in 2001 with a major east-side expansion to be built in 2012. Commentators and city commissioners acknowledged that expanding bus service might be cheaper, but argued for long-term environmental and social benefits, not to mention the ability to kick-start development along the western edge of downtown and in the Pearl District. In the moralistic language often found in contemporary Portland politics, Mayor Vera Katz said in the original debates that "the car will destroy us if we don't come up with innovative solutions."

Compact development and expanding rail service make a difference. Portland workers commute by public transit at a higher rate than residents of most comparable cities, although older cities like Boston, Philadelphia, Washington, and Chicago still rank higher than Portland. More telling is the area-wide decline in vehicle miles traveled (VMT for transportation wonks) by the average Portland-area resident. Running counter to national trends, VMT per person for the Portland-Vancouver region peaked in 1996 at 21.6 miles per day and then dropped to 18.7 by 2008. The decrease in individual driving was great enough that there was a slight drop in total driving miles in 2007 and 2008 despite the area's increasing population.

Transit investment accompanied an economic comeback. Slow recovery from the severe recession of the early 1980s turned into a headlong economic boom in the 1990s. In 1993, *Fortune* found Portland one of the "best cities for knowledge workers." By 1995, *Forbes* magazine could write that "a good quality of life, high immigration levels, and computer smarts helped make this rainy town a winner . . . a town that's far better than most for a young company to be in." Two years later *Time* put Portland on its cover as one of the nation's economic hot spots.

The key to the boom was new vitality in the electronics industry, helping to complete Portland's transition from traditional resource-based manufacturing to high-technology manufacturing and information industries. Several homegrown electronics firms, such as Tektronix and Floating Point, struggled in the rapidly changing marketplace in the 1980s, but the wealth of talent and affordable land made Portland attractive to outside firms in the late 1980s and 1990s. Following Intel's lead, half a dozen major electronics manufacturers announced plans to locate or expand in Portland in 1994–95 alone. The programmed investment totaled more than $10 billion. A significant software industry with specializations in business and engineering applications

Light Rail Passengers. Students leaving the MAX light rail and crossing Portland State University's Urban Plaza. At the heart of the campus, the plaza is flanked by light rail and bus lines, bisected by the Portland Streetcar, and adjacent to the university's bicycling center—all examples of city and regional policies that have encouraged alternatives to automobiles. (Photo by author)

developed to accompany the chip plants and research-and-development fa-cilities. Statewide employment in high-tech companies passed timber-related jobs in 1996—a powerfully symbolic transition after 150 years when farms and forests had been synonymous with Oregon.

The electronics industry touched all corners of the metro area, with major new plants in Gresham and Clark County, but the epicenter was Washington County. The county's employment roughly quadrupled from 1970 to 1996. The Washington County cities of Beaverton, Hillsboro, Tigard, and Tualatin emerged as important centers of employment, retailing, and services. Increas-ingly, business interests in Washington County's "Silicon Forest" chafed at what they saw as Portland-oriented regional policies, arguing unsuccessfully for a western bypass highway to relieve perpetually congested Oregon 217. More companies spun off from the big two—Planar, Merix, and Mentor Graphics from a shrinking Tektronix; RadiSys, Ncube, Sequent, and Lattice Semiconductor from Intel.

The new century was less kind to Oregon high-tech. The fallout from the dot-com bust of 2000-01 illustrated the problem with relying on branch opera-tions and fabrication plants of Asian companies, which were, unfortunately, as easy to close down as to set up. In 2010 Intel remained the most important electronics company; its seven plants and facilities and 15,000 workers made it the metro area's single-largest employer. Despite the downturn, electronic products and computers helped Portland remain a major export center. According to Brookings Institution data, Portland was one of the four metro areas with the fastest growth in value of exports for 2003–08. By the end of that period, it was second in the national arena in the value of exports as a percentage of the metropolitan economy at 21 percent and 13th in total value.

Along with the hardware side of the information economy, Portland continues to be a center for information-using employers. Downtown Portland, with roughly 120,000 jobs, remains the center of finance and business services for the traditional Columbia Basin hinterland. Much of the work in banking, insurance, accounting, and law is straightforward, but the mix includes breakout firms that have national clientele, such as advertising firm Wieden & Kennedy. Portland State University, with 30,000 students in 2010, and OHSU, with nearly $400 million in research funding, were what urban planning specialists term anchor institutions—engines of economic development that are tied to their place by their physical investments and missions.

There was a third, sometimes neglected, element to the 21st-century economy. Embedded in the downtown-neighborhood coalition was an important compromise between old warehousing and manufacturing industries and downtown office employers and developers. Civic leaders know that a seaport and regional trade center needs to push cargo payloads as well as paper. Their compromise has been to use zoning to identify certain parts of the downtown fringe for the expansion of offices and housing (Lloyd District, Pearl-River District) while protecting older uses in other fringe areas through "industrial sanctuary" zoning of older factory and warehouse districts like the Central East Side, Northwest Industrial District, and Swan Island. This is a powerful tool for avoiding the mismatch between the location of jobs and housing that afflicts many metropolitan areas.

The Willamette and Columbia rivers are recreational and environmental amenities, but they are also essential parts of the working economy. The water/rail/energy complex that converges around the lower Willamette has long supported several industrial sectors—especially primary metals, transportation equipment, and machinery manufacturing, not to mention warehousing and distribution. This thick ecology of river-related businesses has one foot planted solidly on the waterfront, but has also thrived in other industrial areas such as northern Clackamas County and the south shore of the Columbia. Indeed, Portland defied the national trend of declining industrial

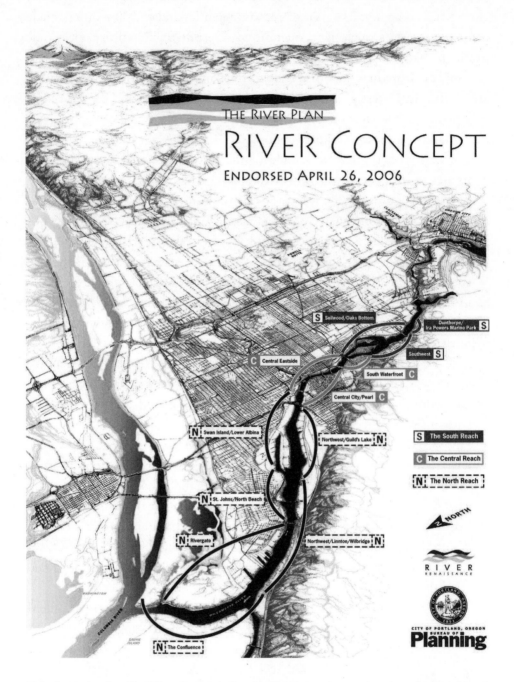

Waterfront planning. The Willamette River in the early 21st century changes character as it passes through the city of Portland. The South Reach is relatively undeveloped, with extensive natural areas such as Oaks Bottom and Ross Island. The Central Reach past downtown is busy with recreation and transportation. Maritime terminals and industry line the North Reach in a delicate balance with the river's natural functions. (Bureau of Planning and Sustainability, City of Portland)

employment, even without counting high-tech companies. The Portland harbor area alone counted 35,000 industrial jobs in the early 21st century. Taken together, the Swan Island-Albina, Northwest, Rivergate, Columbia Corridor, and Milwaukie-Clackamas industrial areas had 147,000 jobs in 2004.

Portland is not Seattle. Its boom times are not as fast and frantic, and its busts are not quite so devastating. Instead, Portland's economic history in the 20th century was one of upticks and plateaus. Decades of growth, such as the 1940s, 1970s, or 1990s, have been followed by periods of consolidation. Putting together the boom of the 1990s, the technology recession of 2001–02, and the following recovery, the Portland metro area had average annual job growth of 2.3 percent (15th among the fifty largest U.S. metro areas). Taking the long perspective, 2010 was another year of consolidation, with more resemblance to 1985 than to 2000.

Even in the midst of economic hard times, Portland was certainly green. The Portland region has received consistently high rankings as a green city in the early 21st century. *Popular Science* named it the greenest city in the country. SustainLane ranked it as the most sustainable U.S. city and the Natural Resources Defense Council put it at number three. Whether Portland will become

Bikes on Esplanade. The Eastbank Esplanade, completed in 2001 and named for Mayor Vera Katz in 2004, connects with Tom McCall Waterfront Park for a three-and-a-half-mile walking and biking loop on both sides of the Willamette River. These participants in the annual "worst day of the year" ride in rainy February are part of Portland's vigorous—even militant—bicycle culture that gives it one of the highest bike commuting rates in the country. (Wikimedia commons)

the Geneva of Sustainability, as promised by some enthusiasts, remains an open question. However, it was one of the leading cities for LEED-certified buildings, not to mention for politicians championing a sustainability agenda.

Portland's reputation and reality as a haven for bicycles and the cyclists who ride them links several trends of recent decades. In the early 1990s, approximately 3,000 bikes crossed the Broadway, Steel, Burnside, and Hawthorne bridges each day. The count doubled to 6,000 by 2000 and tripled to 17,500 in 2010, a rate of increase also shown at non-bridge checkpoints. The popularity of biking has roots in the issue-oriented activism of the 1980s and organizations like the Bicycle Transportation Alliance, but it simultaneously appeals to the earnest newcomers in their twenties and thirties who moved to Portland in disproportionate numbers in the 2000s. Certainly biking for errands and commuting is an environmentally sustainable option. It is also a rain-or-shine activity that expresses, or requires, the Portland love of the outdoors.

Indeed, Portland's natural landscape puts its own unmistakable stamp on the city's character. For the typical Portland resident, a protected environment has meant a usable recreational network of parks, rivers, and mountains. Within a 90-minute drive, Portlanders can enjoy the beaches and headlands of the Pacific shore, the trails of the Cascades and Columbia Gorge, and the ski slopes of Mount Hood—including the country's only late-summer skiing, at Timberline Lodge. Closer to home, Portlanders canoe on the Willamette, sail on the Columbia, jog through the city's fine park system, and generally make use of the outdoors. It seems appropriate that sportswear companies such as Nike, Columbia Sportswear, and Adidas are based in the Portland area, following Jantzen and White Stag from earlier decades.

The state planning system and the urban growth boundary preserve both the agricultural landscape and natural areas, but the metropolitan area also expanded direct public ownership of natural areas. Fearing that private development would overrun the region's remaining hills and stream valleys, voters in 1995 and 2006 approved Metro bond issues totaling $363 million for open space and park acquisition. Winning approval in all three of the core metro counties, the funds purchased more than 10,000 acres through 2010. Oaks Bottom, preserved as a natural area in the 1980s, and Ross Island, a portion transferred to the city as open space in 2008, stood as a mirror and complement to Swan Island. They were a mirror as another set of wetlands and sandbars shaped by the river curving below a crescent of bluffs; a complement as a conserved natural area rather than a transformed industrial area.

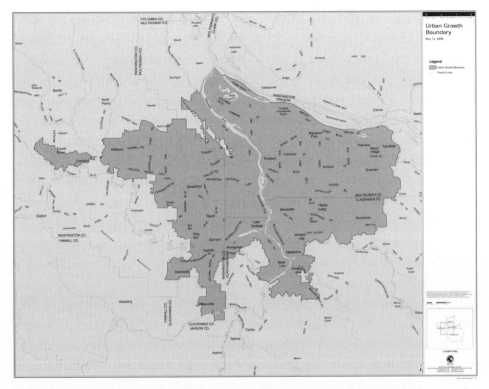

Urban Growth Boundary, as it stood in 2006. The Urban Growth Boundary defines land that is expected to become intensely developed from land that is expected to remain non-urban. Since its establishment in 1978, the UGB has expanded in small increments by a total of just over 10 percent. (Courtesy Metro)

Despite the proliferation of kayaks and mountain bikes, many 21st-century Portlanders also continued to enjoy the outdoors by harvesting its resources, as they had a century earlier. More than 300,000 Oregonians held hunting licenses in 1994; that's more than the number of licenses in the more populous state of Washington and close to the total in California, which has 10 times the population of Oregon. Hunters rise with the stars to track down waterfowl on Sauvie Island or upland birds east of the Cascades. Anglers brave truly nasty weather to catch steelhead and sturgeon. Asian immigrants gather mushrooms and ferns. And the onset of deer season remains an important date for many Portlanders, who have their pickups and campers packed for a Friday-night getaway into the surrounding mountains.

Traditional Portlanders with roots or connections in the historic industrial and natural resource economy temper the region's notoriously progressive politics. Votes on local taxes, on "culture war" issues like gay marriage, and on candidates for state and national office were increasingly polarized on the basis of geography from the 1990s into the new century. Multnomah County was the most liberal in the metropolitan area, voting 75 percent for

Barack Obama in 2008. Its progressive heart throbbed between the West Hills and Mount Tabor, with some precincts voting for liberal candidates and causes by 90 percent or more. The farther east one went in Multnomah County, however, the more Republicans, the more social conservatives, and the more anti-taxers one found. Washington County moved slowly away from its 1980s identity as primarily conservative territory and went 63 percent for Obama. Clackamas County (59 percent) and Columbia County (56 percent) were closer to the political center, and Yamhill County was the most conservative, voting 50–48 for John McCain. Across the river, Clark County (54 percent Obama) and Skamania County (52 percent) were also much more conservative than Portland.

Every savvy politician knows that her future depends as much on the voters who will be moving into her district as on those already there. With this point in mind, the trends in the early 21st century pointed to an increasingly progressive city—and perhaps an increasingly polarized region. Beginning in the 1990s, Portland attracted more than its share of young people with college educations. By 2007, to pick a single year, twice as many 25- to 39-year-olds moved into the metro area as moved out. Results have included a perhaps overly-self-conscious hipster style, plus lots of small entrepreneurs and artisans building upscale bicycles, designing clothing, brewing beer, or roasting coffee. It has developed a vibrant low-key arts scene with plenty of small theater groups; bands and music venues; filmmakers; writers of books, blogs, and zines; and even breakout successes like Dark Horse Comics.

Beneath the trendy surface, Portlanders are conservative about their city. They like what they have and they want to keep it. They like the easy access to the natural Northwest landscape, the human scale of its downtown and neighborhoods, and even—sometimes—the rain. It's been nearly a century and a half since Matthew Deady called Portland the sound, calm alternative to San Francisco. Once he got accustomed to cell phones and talk radio, Deady would find many of the same virtues today in a city whose residents still think it's possible to discern and pursue a public interest that serves entire communities.

There are certainly challenges to a common community of interest, however. Will the "sorting of America" push inner Portland and its outer neighborhoods further apart, or will the political alliance struck between city and suburbs last for another quarter century? Will the hipster and DIY artist generation become engaged as citizens as well as creators and consumers? Will urbanists and environmentalists continue to see mutual benefit in compact metropolitan growth? Will battles over planning details for the Willamette waterfront, transportation improvements, and expansion of the urban growth boundary drive wedges between business and public sector?

In the end, the best way to understand Portland is through its rivers.

The Willamette creates its visual ambiance, flowing high and brown in the late winter and spring, carrying runoff that is twice as great as the entire Colorado River basin. By summer, when the snow has melted from all but the highest peaks, it quiets for fishermen, canoes, and dragon-boat races. High or low, it cuts an open space through the city's center that sets off views from both directions. It is omnipresent in postcard views. From the west, it is the seam that knits together the whole city. From the east bank, it sets off the entire center of Portland at a single glance.

The Columbia made Portland the gateway to the Northwest. It was an avenue of exploration, a pathway for settlement, and an artery of commerce by steamer, railroad, and highway that made—and still makes—Portland the commercial gateway to the interior. Abundant land along the Columbia and Willamette made possible the shipbuilding booms that transformed Portland in the two world wars. Compared with Seattle, Portland is far more deeply embedded in its North American region, less cosmopolitan and worldly, more straightforward and down to earth.

A river is a theme with variations, and so too is Portland's history. A river flows deeper or shallower, cleaner or more polluted. One stretch supports recreation, another nourishes natural systems, and yet another floats the ships of world commerce. But short of geological cataclysm it finds its way, century after century, to the same sea. Portland's themes have appeared and reappeared in the previous chapters—the theme of regionally based commerce and manufacturing, the theme of livable neighborhoods, the theme of gradual ethnic and racial change, and the theme of civic responsibility. C. E. S. Wood meant the inscription that he penned for the Skidmore Fountain—"Good citizens are the riches of a city." Even accounting for the scoundrels and crooks along the way, his fellow Portlanders have continued to believe him.

MT. RAINIER MT. ST. HELENS   MT. ADAMS   **COUNCIL CREST**   MT. HOOD
  Ht. 14556   Ht. 10000   Ht. 12470   **PORTLAND, OREGON**   Ht. 11225
 Dis. 103 miles   Dis. 53 miles   Dis. 75 miles   Dis. 51 miles

Council Crest Amusement Park. From 1907 to 1929, Portlanders could enjoy the Scenic Railway loop and other rides at the amusement park atop 1,073-foot Council Crest. The Big Tree offered stunning views until it was damaged by lightning and replaced with lower observation towers that stood until 1941. (Gholston Collection)

Learning About Portland

Sources and Collections

The best places to begin diving into Portland history are the Portland City Archives and the Oregon Historical Society, conveniently located a few blocks apart at the southern end of downtown. Other important organizations with collections and exhibits on aspects of Portland include the Oregon Jewish Museum, the Oregon Nikkei Legacy Center, the Architectural Heritage Center, and the Special Collections department of the Portland State University library. For regional history, one should also explore the Washington County Museum, the Clackamas County Historical Society and Museum of the Oregon Territory, and other local historical societies and museums.

Web sites and blogs maintained by individuals and organizations have become an important source of images, oral histories, and commentary. The continually growing Oregon Encyclopedia at www.oregonencyclopedia.org is an authoritative online source with many articles dealing with Portland and its region. Other examples include the interesting blog www.cafeunknown.com, the extensive photo archive at www.historicphotoarchive.com, the historic photo blog at www.vintageportland.wordpress.com, and topically focused sites such as www.volgagermans.net/portland and http://www.history.pdx.edu/oaks/oakspg1.htm. Some of my own commentary on Portland is at www.theurbanwest.com.

General Histories and Descriptions

Terrence O'Donnell and Thomas Vaughan, *Portland: A Historical Sketch and Guide* (2nd edition: Portland, 1984) opens with an extended historical essay that tries to capture the character of Portland. Carl Abbott, *Greater Portland: Urban Life and Landscape in the Pacific Northwest* (Philadelphia, 2001) is a more extensive effort to enlist history to illuminate the distinctive characteristics of the Portland metropolitan area. John Trombold and Peter Donahue, *Reading Portland: The City in Prose* (Portland, 2006) is a fascinating collection of contemporary and retrospective writing about Portland in its several centuries.

Harvey Scott's *History of the Oregon Country* edited by Leslie Scott (Cambridge, MA, 1924) and Joseph Gaston's *Portland: Its History and Its Builders* (Chicago, 1911) are records of the city's development by active participants in its history.

Single-volume histories of Portland include Percy Maddux, *City on the Willamette: The Story of Portland, Oregon* (Portland, 1952) and Gordon DeMarco, *A Short History of Portland* (San Francisco, 1990). William Toll's "Commerce, Climate, & Community: A History of Portland & Its People" is another short history available as a set of Web pages at http://www.ohs.org/education/oregonhistory/narratives/histories.cfm. Larry Price, ed., *Portland's Changing Landscape* (Portland, 1987) is a collection of essays on spatial and economic patterns prepared for an annual meeting of the Association of American Geographers in Portland. Connie Ozawa, ed., *The Portland Edge: Challenges and Successes in Growing Communities* (Washington, 2004) is a more recent collection that emphasizes issues of planning and community development.

Three recent "tours" of Portland offer vastly different takes on Portland's history and character: Michael Munk, *The Portland Red Guide: Sites and Stories of Our Radical Past* (Portland, 2007); David Oates, *City Limits: Walking Portland's Urban Growth Boundary* (Corvallis, OR, 2006); and Chuck Palahniuk, *Fugitives and Refugees: A Walk in Portland, Oregon* (New York, 2003).

The Era of Exploration and Settlement

The Native American peoples of western Oregon are treated in Stephen Dow Beckham, *The Indians of Western Oregon* (Coos Bay, OR, 1977) and *Oregon Indians* (Corvallis, 2006); Robert H. Ruby and John A. Brown, *Indians of the Pacific Northwest* (Norman, OK, 1981); and Joel V. Berreman's "Tribal Distribution in Oregon," *Memoirs of the American Anthropological Association*, 47 (1937) discuss native peoples statewide. The people of the lower Columbia are the subject of Robert Ruby and John Brown, *The Chinook Indians: Traders of the Lower Columbia* (Norman, OK, 1976) and Rick Rubin, *Naked Against the Rain: The People of the Lower Columbia River, 1770–1830* (Portland, 1999). Up-to-date scholarly studies include Yvonne P. Hajda, "Regional Social Organization in the Greater Lower Columbia, 1792–1830" (PhD dissertation,

University of Washington, 1984) and Michael Silverstein, "Chinookans of Lower Columbia," in Wayne Suttles, ed., *Northwest Coast*, Vol. 7 of William Sturtevant, ed., *Handbook of North American Indians* (Washington, 1990).

For early exploration and pioneering, the journals of Lewis and Clark (various editions) are an invaluable starting point. Also see: Fred William Powell, *Hall J. Kelley on Oregon* (Princeton, NJ, 1932); Eugene Snyder, *Early Portland: Stump-Town Triumphant* (Portland, 1970); Malcolm Clark, Jr., *The Eden Seekers: The Settlement of Oregon* (Boston, 1981); Howard Corning, *Willamette Landings: Ghost Towns of the River* (Portland, 1973); and William Bowen, *The Willamette Valley: Migration and Settlement on the Oregon Frontier* (Seattle, 1978).

We can examine the perspectives of a 19th-century Portland "insider" in Malcolm Clark, Jr., ed., *Pharisee Among the Philistines: The Diary of Judge Mathew P. Deady, 1871–1892* (Portland, 1975) and an "outsider" in Ruth B. Moynihan, *Rebel for Rights: Abigail Scott Duniway* (New Haven, CT, 1983).

Politics and Policy

Jewel Lansing, *Portland: People, Politics and Power, 1851–2001* (Corvallis, OR, 2002) chronicles the successive City Hall regimes and their accomplishments (or sometimes scandals). E. Kimbark MacColl, *The Growth of a City: Power and Politics in Portland, Oregon, 1915–1950* (Portland, 1978); E. Kimbark MacColl, *The Shaping of a City: Business and Politics in Portland, Oregon, 1885–1915* (Portland, 1976); and E. Kimbark MacColl and Harry Stein, *Merchants, Money and Power: The Portland Establishment 1843–1913* (Portland, 1988) are essential sources for the intertwining of business and politics in the city's first century.

Robert Johnston, *The Radical Middle Class: Populist Democracy and the Question of Capitalism in Progressive Era Portland, Oregon* (Princeton, NJ, 2003) introduces Portland's political tensions and turmoil in the early decades of the 20th century in a prize-winning study. Adam Hodges explores the deep divisions in the era of World War I in "Enemy Aliens and Silk Stocking Girls: The Class Politics of Internment in the Drive for Urban Order During World War I," *Journal of the Gilded Age and Progressive Era*, 6 (October 2007): 431–58; "At War Over the Espionage Act in Portland: Dueling Perspectives from Agent William Bryon and Kathleen O'Brennan," *Oregon Historical Quarterly*, 108 (Fall 2007): 474–86; and "Thinking Globally, Acting Locally: The Portland Soviet and the Emergence of American Communism, 1918–1920," *Pacific Northwest Quarterly*, 98 (Summer 2007): 115–29. Also relevant are Harvey G. Tobie, "Oregon Labor Disputes, 1919–23," *Oregon*

Historical Quarterly 48 (1947) and Kenneth Jackson, *The Ku Klux Klan in the City* (New York, 1967). Paul Pitzer, "Dorothy McCullough Lee: The Successes and Failure of Dottie-Do-Good," *Oregon Historical Quarterly*, 91 (Spring 1990): 5–42 sets the stage for the turmoil of the 1950s. Robert Donnelly, "Organizing Portland: Organized Crime, Municipal Corruption, and the Teamsters Union," *Oregon Historical Quarterly*, 104 (Fall 2003): 334–65 and *Dark Rose: Organized Crime and Corruption in Portland, Oregon* (Seattle, 2011) are scholarly examines of corruption in the 1950s; Phil Stanford, *Portland Confidential: Sex, Crime, and Corruption in the Rose City* (Portland, 2004) is a journalist's take on the same era.

For the transformation of Portland politics since the 1960s, start with Steven Reed Johnson, "The transformation of civic institutions and practices in Portland, Oregon, 1960–1999" (PhD dissertation, Portland State University, 2002). Paul Lewis, *Shaping Suburbia: How Political Institutions Organize Urban Development* (Pittsburgh, 1996) compares the development of regional governance in Portland and Denver. Jeffrey M. Berry, Kent Portnoy, and Ken Thomson, *The Rebirth of Urban Democracy* (Washington, 1993) compares neighborhood activism in Portland with other cities. Howard Hallman, *The Structure and Organization of Neighborhood Councils* (New York, 1977) is an earlier comparative description of the neighborhood association system. Matthew Witt, "Structure and Conflict in Portland's Neighborhood Associations" (PhD dissertation, Portland State University, 2000) critiques the bureaucratic dynamics of neighborhood politics. Matt Love, *The Far Out Story of Vortex I* (Pacific City, OR, 2004) simultaneously demythologizes and celebrates that unique convergence of politics and culture.

Portland figures in Myron Orfield, *Metropolitics* (Washington, 1997) and David Rusk, *Inside Game/Outside Game: Winning Strategies for Saving Urban America* (Washington, 1999). Coalition for a Livable Future, *The Regional Equity Atlas: Metropolitan Portland's Geography of Opportunity* (Portland, 2007) presents data in the Orfield framework. Portland is highlighted in Christopher Leo, "Is Urban Sprawl Back on the Political Agenda: Local Growth Control, Regional Growth Management, and Politics," *Urban Affairs Review*, 34 (1998): 179–211.

Architecture and Planning

Carl Abbott, *Portland: Planning, Politics and Growth in a Twentieth-Century City* (Lincoln, NE, 1983) examines the political setting and results of planning from 1900 through 1980, while Carl Abbott, *The Great Extravaganza: Portland's Lewis and Clark Exposition* (3rd edition: Portland, 2004) describes the first comprehensive world's fair on the Pacific coast. Lisa Blee, "Completing Lewis and Clark's Westward March: Exhibiting a History of Empire at the 1905 Portland World's Fair," *Oregon Historical Quarterly*, 106 (Summer 2005): 232–53; Deborah M. Olsen, "Fair Connections: Women's Separatism and the Lewis and Clark Exposition of 1905," *Oregon Historical Quarterly*, 109 (Summer 2008): 174–203; and Robert Rydell, *All the World's a Fair: Visions of Empire at American International Expositions, 1876–1916* (Chicago, 1984) provide additional perspectives on the fair. Martha Bianco, "Robert Moses and Lewis Mumford: Competing Paradigms of Growth in Portland, Oregon," *Planning Perspectives*, 16 (2001): 95–114 analyzes contrasting ideas about the city's future.

Bart King's *Architectural Guidebook to Portland* (Corvallis, 2007) is an enjoyable starting point. Thomas Vaughan and Virginia Ferriday, eds., *Space, Style and Structure: Building in Northwest America* (Portland, 1974) is a two-volume collection of insightful articles about rural and urban architecture and landscape. Virginia Ferriday, *The Last of the Handmade Buildings: Glazed Terra Cotta in Downtown Portland* (Portland, 1984) examines the early 20th-century buildings that still dominate downtown. Gideon Bosker and Lena Lencek, *Frozen Music: A History of Portland Architecture* (Portland, 1985) offer an idiosyncratic survey of leading architects. There is further detail in Richard Marlitt, *Nineteenth Street* (Portland, 1978); William J. Hawkins III, *The Grand Era of Cast Iron Architecture in Portland* (Portland, 1976); Al Staehli, *Preservation Options for Portland Neighborhoods* (Portland, 1974); Fred DeWolfe, *Portland Tradition in Buildings and People* (Portland, 1980); and Eugene Snyder, *Portland: Names and Neighborhoods* (Portland, 1979). William Hawkins III and William Willingham, *Classic Houses of Portland: 1850–1950* (Portland, 1999) places residential architecture in context, while Philip Niles, *Beauty of the City: A. E. Doyle, Portland's Architect* (Corvallis, OR, 2008) is a biography of perhaps the city's most important local architect. Robert A. Jones, "Re-Presenting the Post-Industrial Neighborhood: Planning and Redevelopment in Portland's Pearl District" (PhD dissertation, Portland State University, 1999) examines the transformation of the downtown fringe into a stylish neighborhood. Randy Gragg, ed., *Where the Revolution Began : Lawrence and Anna Halprin and the Reinvention of Public Space* (Washington, DC , 2009) celebrates the creation and impact of the Lovejoy and Forecourt (Keller) fountains.

For background on Oregon land-use planning, Brent Walth, *Fire at Eden's Gate* (Portland, 1996) is a fast-paced political biography of Tom McCall. Carl Abbott, Deborah Howe, and Sy Adler, *Planning the Oregon Way:*

A Twenty-Year Evaluation (Corvallis, OR, 1994) contains a series of essays on the origins and implementation of the Oregon land-use planning system. Gerrit Knaap and Arthur C. Nelson, *The Regulated Landscape* (Cambridge, MA, 1992) is another examination of Oregon planning. Mark Bello, "Urban Regimes and Downtown Planning in Portland, Oregon and Seattle, Washington, 1972–1992" (PhD dissertation, Portland State University, 1993) examines the politics of downtown planning. Martha Bianco, "Private Profit versus Public Service: Competing Demands in Urban Transportation Policy, Portland, Oregon, 1872–1970" (PhD dissertation, Portland State University, 1994) analyzes the transition from private to public transit. Carl Abbott and Joy Margheim, "Imagining Portland's Urban Growth Boundary: Planning Regulation as Cultural Icon," *Journal of the American Planning Association*, 74 (Spring 2008) and Carl Abbott, "Planning a Sustainable City: The Promise and Performance of Portland's Urban Growth Boundary," in Greg Squires, ed., *Urban Sprawl: Causes, Consequences, and Policy Responses* (Washington, 2002) discuss the impacts of Portland's planning regime.

Social Dynamics

William Toll, *The Making of an Ethnic Middle Class: Portland Jewry over Four Generations* (Albany, NY, 1982), Steve Lowenstein, *The Jews of Oregon, 1850–1950* (Portland, 1987), and Scott Cline, "The Jews of Oregon: A Statistical Dimension, 1860–1880," *Oregon Historical Quarterly*, 88 (Spring 1987): 5–26 examine ethnic assimilation. Toll's careful research is also available in "Permanent Settlement: Japanese Families in Portland in 1920," *Western Historical Quarterly*, 28 (Spring 1997): 19–44. A valuable overview of Portland's development as a community during the 19th century is Paul Merriam's "Portland, 1840–1890: A Social and Economic History" (PhD dissertation, University of Oregon, 1971).

The African American experience is explored in Albert Broussard, "McCants Stewart: The Struggles of a Black Attorney in the Urban West," *Oregon Historical Quarterly*, 89 (Summer 1988): 157–80; William Toll, "Black Families and Migration to a Multiracial Society: Portland, Oregon, 1900–1924," *Journal of American Ethnic History*, 17 (Spring 1998); Rudy Pearson, "A Menace to the Neighborhood: Housing and African Americans in Portland, 1941–45," *Oregon Historical Quarterly*, 102 (Summer 2001): 158–79; Kimberly Mangun, *A Force for Change: Beatrice Morrow Cannady and the Struggle for Civil Rights in Oregon, 1912–1936* (Corvallis, 2010); Ethan Johnson and Felicia Williams, "Desegregation and Multiculturalism in Portland Public Schools," *Oregon Historical Quarterly*, 111 (Spring 2010): 6–37; and Jules Boykoff and

Martha Gies, "'We're Going to Defend Ourselves:' The Portland Chapter of the Black Panther Party and Local Media Response," *Oregon Historical Quarterly*, 111 (Fall 2010): 278–311.

For early law enforcement, see Charles A. Tracy, "The Police Function in Portland, 1851–74," *Oregon Historical Quarterly*, 80 (1979) and Gloria Myers, *A Municipal Mother: Portland's Lola Green Baldwin, America's First Policewoman* (Corvallis, OR, 1995). Peter Boag, *Same-Sex Affairs: Constructing and Controlling Homosexuality in the Pacific Northwest* (Berkeley, CA, 2003) examines the conflicting ways in which Portlanders understood and regulated sexual activity.

Amy Kesselman, *Fleeting Opportunities: Women Shipyard Workers in Portland and Vancouver during World War II and Reconversion* (Albany, NY, 1990) and Manly Maben, *Vanport* (Portland, 1987) explore the social impacts of World War II. Vanport also features in Dolores Hayden, *Redesigning the American Dream* (New York, 1984) and Heather Fryer, *Perimeters of Democracy: Inverse Utopians and the Wartime Social Landscape in the American West* (Lincoln, NE, 2010). Tanya Lyn March, "Guild's Lake Courts: An Impermanent Housing Project" (PhD dissertation, Portland State University, 2010) examines the city's other massive World War II housing project. Stuart McElderry, "Vanport Conspiracy Rumors and Social Relations in Portland, 1940–1950," *Oregon Historical Quarterly*, 99 (Summer 1998): 134–63 places the Vanport flood in the context of racial relations.

Chris D. Sawyer, "From Whitechapel to Old Town: The Life and Death of the Skid Row District, Portland, Oregon" (PhD dissertation, Portland State University, 1984) looks at the residential environment of transient workers. Marie Rose Wong, *Sweet Cakes, Long Journey: The Chinatowns of Portland, Oregon* (Seattle, 2004) looks at the Asian immigrants who occupied much of the same territory. Robert Dietsche, *Jumptown: The Golden Years of Portland Jazz, 1942–57* (Corvallis, OR, 2005) focuses on African Americans, while William W. Pilcher, *The Portland Longshoremen: A Dispersed Urban Community* (New York, 1972) is an ethnographic study of a portion of the white working class.

For recent decades, Robert Richard White, "Faith, Hope and Leverage: Attributes of Effective Faith-Based Community Organizations" (PhD dissertation, Portland State University, 1996) examines the Albina Ministerial Alliance and Portland Organizing Project. Elinor Langer, *A Hundred Little Hitlers* (New York, 2003) examines the white supremacist minority in 1990s Portland. Jessica Morrell, *Voices from the Street: Truths about Homelessness from Sisters of the Road* (Portland, 2007) contains the voices of marginal and homeless Portlanders—a sort of mirror of Langer's subjects. The Coalition for a Livable Future developed *The Regional Equity Atlas: Metropolitan Portland's Geography of Opportunity* (Portland, 2007) with the assistance of Portland State University.

Economic Development

Glenn Quiett, *They Built the West: An Epic of Rails and Cities* (New York, 1934) and Arthur Throckmorton, *Oregon Argonauts: Merchant Adventurers on the Western Frontier* (Portland, 1961) describe key economic actors and decisions in the 19th century.

For the more recent Portland economy, see Tom Harvey, "Portland, Oregon: Regional City in a Global Economy," *Journal of Urban Geography*, 17 (1996): 95–114; Gordon Dodds and Craig Wollner, *The Silicon Forest: High Tech in the Portland Area, 1945–1985* (Portland, 1990); Chris Ertel, "Running in Place: Economic Growth and Income Stagnation in Portland, Oregon, 1983–1993" (PhD dissertation, University of California, Berkeley, 1997); and Heike Mayer, "Taking Root in the Silicon Forest: The Role of High Technology Firms as Surrogate Universities in Portland, Oregon" (PhD dissertation, Portland State University, 2003); and Heike Mayer, "Planting High-Technology Seeds: Tektronix's Role in the Creation of Portland's Silicon Forest," *Oregon Historical Quarterly*, 106 (Winter 2005): 568–93. Charles Heying, et al., *Brew to Bikes: Portland's Artisan Economy* (Portland, 2010) examines the growing low-tech economy. Current demographic and economic data is also found in *Metroscape*, a periodical published by the Institute for Portland Metropolitan Studies at Portland State University. Several of the essays in Price, *Portland's Changing Landscape*, are also useful.

Portland's Place in Its Region

The history of Portland has been well served by several studies that place the development of the city within the growth of the Pacific Northwest. Dorothy Johansen and Charles Gates, *Empire of the Columbia* (New York, 1967) and Earl Pomeroy, *The Pacific Slope* (New York, 1965) are older but deeply researched regional surveys. Gordon Dodds, *Oregon: A Bicentennial History* (New York, 1977); David Peterson Del Mar, *Oregon's Promise* (Corvallis, OR, 2003), and William Robbins, *Oregon: This Storied Land* (Portland, 2005) are single-volume state histories. Samuel Dicken, *The Making of Oregon* (Portland, 1979) gives a geographical perspective. William Robbins, *Landscapes of Promise: The Oregon Story, 1800–1940* (Seattle, 1997) and *Landscapes of*

Conflict, The Oregon Story, 1940–2000 (Seattle, 2004) are environmental histories in which Portland plays a prominent role.

Richard White, *The Organic Machine: The Remaking of the Columbia River* (New York, 1995) provides a broad context for understanding the changing economic roles of the Columbia. Charles McKinley, *Uncle Sam in the Pacific Northwest: Federal Management of Natural Resources in the Pacific Northwest* (Berkeley, CA, 1952) describes federal intervention during the first half of the century. William Dietrich, *Northwest Passage: The Great Columbia River* (Seattle, 1996) surveys the history and status of the river and its basin. Carl Abbott, Sy Adler, and Margery Post Abbott, *Planning a New West: The Columbia River Gorge National Scenic Area* (Corvallis, OR, 1997) examines an innovative planning effort in the immediate environs of Portland. Gail Wells, *The Tillamook: A Created Forest Comes of Age* (Corvallis, OR, 1999) tells the story of the great Tillamook burn and its aftermath.

Index